Meat Meals in Minutes

A Benjamin Company Book

Cover Photo: Sweet and Sour Green Beans (page 79), Bacon 'n Cheese Baked Potatoes (page 86), Baked SPAM (page 109)

Home Economist:	Beatrice Cihak
Editor:	Cathy Silver
Photography:	Walter Storck
Typography:	A-Line, Milwaukee
Production:	Beth Kukkonen
Art and Design:	Tom Brecklin

Prepared and produced by The Benjamin Company, Inc.
485 Madison Avenue
New York, New York 10022

ISBN: 0-87502-085-2
Library of Congress Card Catalog Number: 80-69809

Printed in the United States of America
First Printing: February, 1981

Table of Contents

In 1891, Mr. George A. Hormel started his company with three personal goals: quality, wholesomeness, and flavor. In those days, Mr. Hormel and a handful of employees produced ham, bacon, sausage, and fresh meat. Today, over 8,000 men and women employed by the Hormel Company in Austin, Minnesota, maintain George A. Hormel's highest standards in over 750 products. The company has grown into one of the nation's leading meat packers and food processors, but its promise to the consumer remains the same.

The Hormel Company's dedication to fine foods began with its founder. George A. Hormel was born in 1860 in Buffalo, New York. At the age of 13, he left school and found a job lathing wood to help support his family. He was the oldest of 12 living children, and the economic panic of 1873 had forced the closing of his father's tannery business. Three years later, George went to Chicago to work for an uncle who ran a packinghouse market. By the time he was 19 or 20, George had enough tannery and packinghouse experience to land a job buying hides. The Midwest territory assigned to him included Austin, Minnesota, then a town of 3,000 people.

In 1887, Austin welcomed the opening of Friedrich & Hormel, Butchers and Packers, known for "Fresh and salt meats, fish and game in season. Satisfaction guaranteed. Goods delivered free." Partner Albrecht Friedrich ran the retail side, while George Hormel supervised the production of sausage, ham, bacon, and other meat. Production quickly outpaced the retail trade; so the firm began to sell to other retailers in surrounding communities. Business was so good that within two years an extension to the building was needed and constructed. A steam packinghouse was added in 1889, and in 1891 Friedrich & Hormel supplied an order for two carloads of hides weighing nearly 55,000 pounds, a record-breaking shipment at that time.

When the partnership was dissolved in 1891, Friedrich retained the retail market and Hormel the production facilities. The town of Austin continued to boast the newly formed George A. Hormel & Company. It was one of only four small packers in the area to survive the panic of 1893, when nationwide financial disaster was compounded by competition brought in on the new refrigerated railway cars.

To survive and prosper, George Hormel knew he had to introduce more and better products. His philosophy was, "Innovate, don't imitate." In 1927, Hormel featured the first canned ham in the country. Hormel Chili Con Carne was successfully introduced in 1935, as were the first items in the Dinty Moore product line: Beef Stew, Corned Beef and Cabbage, Spaghetti and Meat Balls, and Irish Stew.

In 1937, after a long period of testing and development, Hormel was ready to promote a special spiced meat product composed of ham with some pork shoulder meat. But the tasty innovation lacked a catchy label; so the company offered a $100 reward for an appropriate brand name. Actor Kenneth Daigneau, the brother of a Hormel executive, supplied the winning entry — SPAM.

Since that time, SPAM has won everyone's vote for favorite luncheon meat. Over three billion cans of SPAM have been manufactured; in recent years, one hundred million cans were sold annually. During World War II, enormous quantities of SPAM were sent abroad to ease food shortages, prompting a retired British diplomat to comment in later years, "As a youngster I always thought that Churchill together with SPAM won the war for the Allies!"

Continuing the tradition begun by George A. Hormel, SPAM and other fine Hormel products ensure quality, convenience, and economy. They provide welcome and delicious family meals and delightful company fare. In this book, you will find many ways to enjoy the versatility of Hormel products. There are breakfast and brunch favorites, dinner entrées, vegetable side dishes, one-pot meals, salads, sandwiches, soups, and snacks. One chapter is devoted to wonderful party recipes; another features cooking shortcuts for camping, picnics, and busy days year-round. Enjoy them all, on every occasion, with very best wishes from Hormel.

Good Morning!

What's your favorite wake-up? A sunny morning platter of Savory Egg Scramble? The rise-and-shine aroma of Sausage Pancakes? A hot Roast Beef Hash Bake to warm up the day? If you like your breakfast fast and nutritious, you'll choose an omelet from this chapter — Western, Bacon 'n Cheese, Puffed Hash, or Tamale. If it's a change of pace that gets you started, you'll rally to Ranchero Eggs, Corn Fritters, and Corned Beef Mini-Loaves. And if your idea of pleasure is a leisurely brunch, here is a selection worth lingering over — from Frittata and Towers of Bagels to Spinach Soufflé Crêpes and Elegant Quiche.

Ranchero Eggs   4 Servings

Add a little spice to your morning with this Mexican favorite.

1 large onion, thinly sliced	1 teaspoon chili powder
1/4 cup chopped green pepper	1/4 teaspoon oregano
2 tablespoons cooking oil	4 eggs
1 can (16 ounces) tomatoes, broken up	2 slices American cheese, quartered
1 can (7 ounces) SPAM, diced	

In large skillet, sauté onion and green pepper in oil until onion is transparent. Add tomatoes, SPAM, chili powder, and oregano; bring to a boil. Lower heat and simmer 15 minutes, stirring occasionally. Push solids aside in 4 equally spaced places in skillet; break an egg into each space. Cover and cook about 15 minutes or until eggs are just set; place 2 cheese quarters on each egg; cover and cook about 5 minutes longer until cheese melts and eggs are cooked to desired consistency.

Savory Egg Scramble

6 Servings

This dish is colorful, too, thanks to green peppers, chives, and parsley.

1/4 cup butter or margarine
1/2 cup chopped onion
1/2 cup chopped green pepper
  1 can (8 ounces) potatoes,
    drained and sliced
  1 teaspoon fresh or frozen
    chopped chives

12 eggs
1/2 teaspoon salt
1/8 teaspoon pepper
1/4 cup Hormel Bacon Bits
1/4 cup chopped parsley

Melt butter in large skillet; sauté onion, green pepper, potatoes, and chives over low heat until onions are transparent. Beat eggs, salt, and pepper; mix in bacon and parsley. Pour into skillet. Cook over low heat, stirring constantly until eggs reach desired consistency.

Tamale Omelet

3 Servings

Tamales and eggs create a breakfast fiesta!

1 can Hormel Tamales
6 eggs, divided
3/4 teaspoon salt, divided
  Pepper

3 tablespoons butter or
  margarine, divided
  Cheddar cheese,
  shredded

Remove tamales from can and while wrappers are still on them heat gently in small flat pan. Remove wrappers and leave tamales in pan to keep warm. To prepare each omelet, beat together 2 eggs, 1/4 teaspoon salt, and dash pepper. Melt 1 tablespoon butter in small skillet; pour eggs into it. Cook over low heat, pulling cooked edges of omelet back into center as set. Tilt and turn skillet as necessary to let uncooked portion flow toward edges. When eggs are set but moist, place 2 tamales on omelet; fold half over to cover other half. Slide onto serving plate. Repeat to make three omelets. Sprinkle each omelet with cheese.

Nice to know: Hot and Spicy Beef Tamales will taste terrific in this omelet, too.

Puffed Hash Omelet

4 Servings

Crown a regal puffed omelet rich with melted cheese.

6 eggs
2 tablespoons water
1/4 teaspoon salt
Dash pepper
1 tablespoon butter or
margarine
1 can (15 ounces) Mary
Kitchen Roast Beef
Hash

1/3 cup chopped green
pepper
1/2 teaspoon chili powder
1/2 cup shredded Monterey
Jack cheese

Combine eggs, water, salt, and pepper until well blended. Melt butter in large omelet pan or skillet; pour in egg mixture. Cook over low heat, pushing edges in toward center as mixture sets. Tilt and turn pan as necessary to allow uncooked portion to flow to the edge. When mixture is set but surface is still moist, slide omelet onto oven-proof plate or cookie sheet. Combine hash, green pepper, and chili powder; spoon evenly over top of omelet. Bake in 400°F oven 10 minutes. Sprinkle with cheese; bake 5 minutes longer.

Bacon 'n Cheese Omelet

2 Servings

Worth waking up for — bacon 'n eggs at their best!

1/2 cup (about 2 ounces)
shredded Cheddar cheese
2 tablespoons Hormel Bacon
Bits
1 teaspoon fresh or
frozen chopped chives

4 eggs
1 tablespoon milk
1/4 teaspoon salt
Pepper to taste
1 tablespoon butter or
margarine

Combine cheese, bacon, and chives; reserve. Beat eggs until well mixed; stir in milk, salt, and pepper. Melt butter in 10-inch omelet pan or skillet; pour in egg mixture. Cook over medium heat, pushing cooked edges in toward center and tilting pan to let uncooked portions flow to edges. When top is set but still moist, sprinkle cheese and bacon mixture over half the omelet. Flip uncovered half of omelet over cheese-topped half. Cook until cheese melts and omelet is browned on bottom. Slide onto serving plate; cut in half to serve.

Roast Beef Hash Bake
6 Servings

Hearty and attractive — a hash 'n egg "pie" rimmed with ripe red tomatoes. This is an after-the-game brunch or hearty breakfast.

1 large tomato	1/4 cup chopped onion
2 cans (15 ounces each) Mary Kitchen Roast Beef Hash	6 eggs

Cut tomato in 6 slices; halve each slice. Stand tomatoes around edge of lightly-greased 10-inch pie plate. Combine hash and onion; spoon into pie plate. Bake in 375°F oven 10 minutes. Remove from oven. Make 6 equally-spaced depressions in hash; break an egg into each depression. Lower heat to 325°F; bake about 25 minutes, or until eggs are cooked to desired doneness.

Western Omelet
4 Omelets

A luscious omelet full of "home on the range" flavor.

1 large green pepper, seeded and chopped	8 eggs, divided
2 medium onions, thinly sliced	4 tablespoons milk, divided
2 tablespoons cooking oil	1/2 teaspoon salt, divided
1 can (7 ounces) SPAM, diced	Pepper to taste
1/4 teaspoon chili powder	4 teaspoons butter or margarine, divided

In medium skillet, sauté green pepper and onions in oil until slightly browned. Stir in SPAM and chili powder until well mixed. For each omelet, beat together 2 eggs, 1 tablespoon milk, 1/8 teaspoon salt, and pepper. In 8- or 9-inch omelet pan or skillet, heat 1 teaspoon butter until hot, and pour in egg mixture. Cook over medium heat, pushing to center cooked edges of omelet as egg sets and tilting pan to allow uncooked mixture to run to edges. When surface of omelet is set, spoon 1/2 cup SPAM mixture on half of omelet; flip uncovered half over filling. When bottom of omelet is browned slide onto serving plate. Repeat to make 4 omelets.

Frittata

6 Servings

It's an upside-down omelet, a festive egg "cake" — in Italy it's called a Frittata.

1/2 cup coarsely chopped onion
1/2 cup coarsely chopped
        green pepper
   3 tablespoons cooking oil,
        divided
   1 can (7 ounces) SPAM, diced
   2 medium potatoes, cooked,
        peeled, and cubed

  10 pitted black olives,
        chopped
   6 eggs
   2 tablespoons water
1/4 teaspoon salt
        Pepper to taste

In 10-inch omelet pan or skillet, sauté onion and green pepper in 2 tablespoons oil until lightly browned. Add SPAM, potatoes, and olives; cook over low heat 5 minutes stirring often. Loosen food from bottom of pan; add remaining oil. Tilt pan to cover bottom. Mix eggs, water, salt, and pepper; pour over SPAM mixture. Cover and cook over low heat 15 minutes or until egg is set on top. With pancake turner, loosen edges and bottom; invert onto serving platter.

Towers of Bagels

6 Sandwiches

Sliced bagels and three tempting fillings stack up as a great entertaining idea.

   2 tablespoons cooking oil
   1 tablespoon vinegar
1/4 teaspoon sugar
1/8 teaspoon salt
        Pepper to taste

   1 small cucumber, washed,
        unpeeled, and sliced
   6 bagels
   1 can (12 ounces) SPAM
   3 ounces Boursin cheese

Combine oil, vinegar, sugar, salt, and pepper. Add cucumber; cover and refrigerate at least 1 hour. Carefully cut bagels crosswise into 4 slices; cut SPAM into 12 slices. To make towers overlap 2 slices SPAM on bottom slice of each bagel. Spread next slice with cheese. Drain cucumbers; place on third slice of bagel. Top with remaining bagel slices.

Nice to know: If Boursin cheese is not available, make your own by mixing together a 3-ounce package cream cheese, 1 tablespoon milk, and 1/4 teaspoon each garlic powder, dillweed, and oregano.

Biscuit Roll

6 Servings

Elegance with ease — a change-of-pace brunch roll that starts with biscuit mix.

1 can (12 ounces) SPAM
1 cup dairy sour cream, divided
1/2 cup frozen green peas, thawed
2 cups biscuit mix

2 teaspoons crumbled dehydrated onion flakes
1/2 cup plus 2 tablespoons milk, divided
1 tablespoon prepared horseradish

Grind SPAM or process in food processor until smooth. Stir in 1/3 cup sour cream and peas; reserve. In bowl, combine biscuit mix and onion flakes; add 1/2 cup milk. Stir just until dough forms a ball. Turn out on lightly-floured surface; knead 10 to 20 times. Roll or pat out on floured surface to a 12×9-inch rectangle; spread with SPAM mixture. Roll up jelly-roll fashion, beginning at long end; pinch dough together to seal. Place on greased baking sheet, seam side down; brush with 1 tablespoon milk. Bake in 400°F oven about 25 minutes, or until browned. Meanwhile, combine remaining sour cream, 1 tablespoon milk, and horseradish. Cut roll into slices to serve and top with dollop of horseradish sauce.

Corn Fritters

18 Fritters

Crisp, golden mouthwatering treats.

1 cup flour
1 teaspoon baking powder
1/4 teaspoon salt
2 eggs
1/4 cup milk
1 tablespoon cooking oil

1 can (7 ounces) SPAM, diced
1 package (10 ounces) frozen whole-kernel corn, cooked and drained
Shortening

Stir together flour, baking powder, and salt until well mixed; reserve. In medium bowl, beat eggs with milk until frothy; stir in oil. Add flour mixture; stir just until flour is moistened. Gently mix in SPAM and corn. Drop batter by heaping tablespoonfuls into shortening heated to 375°F. Fry until browned, turning as needed. Drain on paper towels. Serve with warm maple or buttered pancake syrup.

Corned Beef Mini-Loaves   2 Servings

Shape and bake a great new look for corned beef hash.

1 egg
1 can (15 ounces) Mary
     Kitchen Corned Beef
     Hash
2 tablespoons finely
     chopped onion

2 tablespoons drained
     pickle relish
3 tablespoons packaged
     bread crumbs, divided
   Butter or margarine

In medium bowl, beat egg until frothy. Mix in hash, onion, relish, and 1 tablespoon bread crumbs. Generously spread butter inside two 12-ounce heatproof cups; liberally sprinkle remaining bread crumbs. Divide corned beef mixture into cups, packing down firmly. Bake in 400°F oven 20 to 25 minutes, or until hot. Remove from oven; let stand 5 minutes. Unmold onto serving plates.

Iowa Corn Pudding   8 Servings

A one-pot bonanza for Sunday brunch.

2 tablespoons butter or
     margarine
1/3 cup chopped green pepper
1/4 cup chopped onion
6 eggs
2 cups milk
1 tablespoon flour
2 teaspoons sugar

1 teaspoon salt
1/8 teaspoon pepper
1 can (12 ounces) SPAM
2 packages (10 ounces
     each) frozen whole-
     kernel corn, thawed
     and drained

Melt butter in medium skillet; sauté green pepper and onion until tender; remove from heat. In medium bowl, beat eggs slightly; stir in milk. Mix flour, sugar, salt, and pepper; stir into vegetables; reserve. Cut SPAM in 8 slices; place on bottom of greased 12×8×2-inch baking dish. Sprinkle corn over SPAM. Pour in custard mixture. Bake in 300°F oven 1 hour and 10 minutes, or until softly set. Cut into squares to serve.

Spinach Soufflé Crêpes
8 Servings

A most impressive dish: Feather-light crêpes filled with spinach soufflé and topped with a creamy cheese sauce.

2 eggs	1 can (12 ounces) SPAM
1/2 cup flour	1 package (12 ounces)
1/4 teaspoon salt	frozen spinach soufflé,
3/4 cup milk	slightly thawed
Butter or margarine,	Cheese Sauce (below)
divided	

In small bowl, beat eggs. Add flour and salt; mix until smooth. Slowly add milk. Melt 1 tablespoon butter; stir into batter. Cover and refrigerate at least 1 hour.

To make crêpes, heat 8-inch omelet pan until hot; add 1/2 teaspoon butter. Pour in a scant 1/4 cup batter; tilt and turn pan to spread batter evenly over bottom. Bake until lightly browned on bottom; turn to brown other side. Repeat to make 8 crêpes.

Cut SPAM into 8 long pieces; cut each piece in half lengthwise. To assemble crêpes, place 2 strips SPAM on each crêpe; top with 1/4 cup spinach soufflé; roll up loosely. Place in lightly greased baking dish, seam side down. Repeat with remaining crêpes. Bake in 400°F oven 20 minutes. Pour Cheese Sauce over top; bake 5 minutes longer.

Nice to know: Crêpes can be prepared the night before, stacked between sheets of waxed paper, and refrigerated until you're ready to fill them.

Cheese Sauce

1 tablespoon butter or	3/4 cup milk
margarine	1/4 teaspoon Worcestershire
1 tablespoon flour	sauce
1/8 teaspoon salt	1/2 cup (2 ounces)
1/8 teaspoon dry mustard	grated sharp
Pepper to taste	Cheddar cheese

In small saucepan, melt butter; blend in flour, salt, mustard, and pepper. Add milk and Worcestershire; stir until smooth. Cook and stir over medium heat until mixture thickens and boils. Add cheese; stir over low heat just until cheese melts.

Corny Pancakes

12 Pancakes

A "corny" breakfast trick that never fails to win smiles.

1 1/2 cups pancake mix
   1 cup milk
   1 can (8 ounces) cream-style
      corn

1 egg
1 tablespoon cooking oil
1 can (7 ounces) SPAM,
   finely chopped

In medium bowl, combine pancake mix, milk, corn, egg, and oil. Stir in SPAM. Using 1/3 cup for each pancake, pour batter on greased griddle and bake over medium heat until browned on bottom. Turn and brown other side. Serve with maple or buttered pancake syrup or honey.

Surprise-Inside Cassolets

4 Servings

Delightfully different — complete meal mini-casseroles.

   6 eggs, divided
1/4 cup catsup
   2 teaspoons dehydrated
      onion flakes
   2 cans (15 ounces each) Mary
      Kitchen Roast Beef Hash

2 tablespoons packaged
   bread crumbs
Mustard Sauce (below)

Hard-cook 4 eggs. Shell; set aside. In medium bowl, beat 2 eggs; mix in catsup and onion flakes. Stir in hash. Lightly butter four 8 oz. heatproof cups; dust with bread crumbs. Spoon a little hash mixture into bottom of each baking cup; set 1 hard-cooked egg in each cup. Spoon remaining hash into cups to cover eggs completely. Bake each cup in 375°F oven about 20 minutes. Serve hot with Mustard Sauce.

Mustard Sauce

2 tablespoons butter or
   margarine
2 tablespoons flour
4 teaspoons prepared
   mustard

1 teaspoon Worcester-
   shire sauce
3/4 teaspoon salt
   Dash pepper
1 cup milk

In small saucepan, melt butter. Blend in flour, mustard, Worcestershire, salt, and pepper. Mix in milk. Cook and stir over medium heat until mixture thickens and boils. Serve hot.

Yam-Apple Scallop

4 to 6 Servings

Old-fashioned goodness in a breezy preparation.

2 packages (12 ounces each)
  scalloped apples, thawed
1 can (16 ounces) yams

1 can (12 ounces) SPAM
2 tablespoons honey or
  pancake syrup

Spread apples over bottom of lightly-greased 10-inch square baking dish. Drain yams; place around edges of dish. Cut SPAM into 6 slices; overlap in center. Drizzle honey over SPAM and yams. Bake in 400°F oven 20 to 25 minutes, or until hot.

Microwave directions: Assemble casserole as above. Microwave 11 minutes turning casserole 1/4 turn after 4 and 7 minutes. Cover and let stand 5 minutes.

Ratatouille Pie

6 Servings

As sunny as the south of France — a beautiful French vegetable medley baked in a whole-meal pie.

2 zucchini (1 pound)
1 eggplant (1 pound), cubed
3 tablespoons cooking oil
1 large green pepper,
  seeded and coarsely
  chopped
1 large onion, coarsely
  chopped
2 cloves garlic, minced
1 large tomato, peeled and
  coarsely chopped

1/2 teaspoon thyme
1/4 teaspoon salt
1/4 teaspoon pepper
1 bay leaf
1 can (7 ounces) SPAM,
  diced
Pastry for 2-crust
  9-inch pie

Halve zucchini lengthwise; cut into 1-inch pieces. In large skillet, sauté eggplant and zucchini in oil 5 minutes, stirring often. Mix in green pepper, onion, and garlic; cook 5 minutes, stirring often. Mix in tomato, thyme, salt, pepper, and bay leaf. Cover and simmer 15 minutes. Add SPAM; cook, uncovered, 15 minutes longer. Let cool slightly. Roll out half of pastry to fit 9-inch pie plate; fill with SPAM mixture. Cover with remaining pastry; seal and flute edges. Make several slits in top crust. Bake in 425°F oven 20 minutes. Lower heat to 375°F and bake 15 minutes longer, or until lightly browned.

Sausage Pancakes

12 Pancakes

So rich, so satisfying, so easy!

1 can (5 ounces) Hormel
　Vienna Sausages
1 box (8 1/2 ounces) corn
　muffin mix

1 egg
2 tablespoons melted
　shortening
3/4 cup milk

Slice each sausage into 6 pieces; reserve. Combine remaining ingredients in small bowl; mix until dry ingredients are moistened (batter will be slightly lumpy). Using a scant 1/4 cup batter for each pancake, pour batter onto lightly-greased hot griddle. Set 3 or 4 sausage slices into each pancake; cook until bubbles appear and edges begin to dry. Turn to brown other side. Serve with syrup.

Bacon 'n Cheddar Biscuits

12 Biscuits

Bake hot biscuits even better with Cheddar cheese and bacon.

2 cups biscuit mix
1/3 cup shredded Cheddar
　cheese

3 tablespoons Hormel
　Bacon Bits
1/2 cup water

Stir all ingredients together to form a soft dough; shape into ball. Knead 5 times on lightly-floured surface. Roll out 1/2-inch thick. Cut with floured 2-inch cutter. Place biscuits on ungreased cookie sheet. Bake in 450°F oven 8 to 10 minutes until lightly browned. Serve warm.

Sausage Pancakes, Bacon 'n Cheddar Biscuits

Elegant Quiche

2 9-inch Quiche

Always welcomed by guests — delicate, custard-rich quiche.

2 frozen 9-inch pie crusts,
  thawed
1 can (12 ounces) SPAM,
  finely diced
1 cup (4 ounces) grated
  Swiss cheese
2 tablespoons grated
  Parmesan cheese

5 eggs
2 cups half and half
1/2 cup milk
1/4 teaspoon salt
  Pepper to taste
  Nutmeg

Bake pie crusts in 400°F oven 5 minutes; remove. Increase oven heat to 425°F. Divide and sprinkle the SPAM and cheeses into each crust. Beat eggs; stir in half-and-half, milk, salt, and pepper. Pour over mixture in crust. Sprinkle with nutmeg. Bake 15 minutes. Lower heat to 350°F and bake 10 minutes longer, or until top is browned and custard lightly set. Let stand 5 minutes before cutting.

Nice to know: Unbaked quiche freezes well, so you can save one for another day.

Speedy Quiche

1 10-inch Quiche

A wonderful pie for breakfast, lunch or later-on snacking.

1 can (7 ounces) SPAM, cubed
1/4 cup chopped onion
1/4 cup chopped green pepper
1 tablespoon cooking oil
1 cup (about 4 ounces)
    shredded Monterey Jack
    cheese

2 cups milk
1 cup biscuit mix
4 eggs
1/8 teaspoon pepper

In medium skillet, sauté SPAM, onion, and green pepper in oil until vegetables are tender, stirring often. Spoon mixture into lightly-greased 10-inch pie plate; sprinkle with cheese. Combine remaining ingredients in blender or food processor; blend until smooth, or beat with hand mixer about 1 minute. Pour evenly into pie plate. Bake in 400°F oven about 30 minutes, or until knife inserted in center comes out clean. Let stand 5 minutes before cutting.

Nice to know: You can substitute a 12-ounce can of SPAM, using 7 ounces as indicated in the recipe. The additional SPAM can be sliced and placed on top for the last 5 minutes of baking.

Glazed Ham

6 to 8 Servings

Highlight a party brunch with this tangy glazed ham. Complete the festive menu with Savory Egg Scramble (page 8) and Bacon 'n Cheddar Biscuits (page 18).

3 pound Hormel Ham
1/4 cup firmly packed light
    brown sugar

1 tablespoon prepared
    mustard
1 teaspoon Worcestershire
    sauce

Place ham on rack in baking pan. Bake in 325°F oven 45 minutes. Stir together sugar, mustard, and Worcestershire until smooth; spoon over ham. Bake about 30 minutes longer until internal temperature reaches 130°F, brushing twice more with mustard mixture.

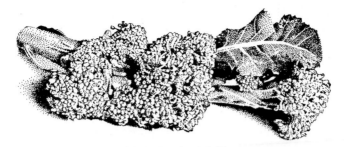

Broccoli Soufflé

4 Servings

Everybody loves a high-rising soufflé — especially when there's no guesswork involved.

2 tablespoons chopped green onion	1 package (10 ounces) frozen chopped broccoli, thawed
3 tablespoons butter or margarine	1 can (12 ounces) SPAM, cut into chunks
3 tablespoons flour	
Pepper to taste	1/4 teaspoon salt
1 cup milk	1/4 teaspoon cream of tartar
4 eggs, separated	
2 tablespoons grated Parmesan cheese	

Butter bottom of 1 1/2-quart soufflé dish. Tie an aluminum foil collar of double thickness around dish, extending 2 inches above top. In medium saucepan, sauté onions in butter until transparent; blend in flour and pepper. Stir in milk; cook and stir over medium heat until mixture thickens and boils. Beat egg yolks slightly; stir in a little of the hot mixture. Add yolks to saucepan with cheese; cook and stir over low heat until mixture thickens. Remove from heat. Place broccoli and SPAM in food processor; use chopping blade and process until finely chopped (or finely chop by hand); stir into sauce mixture. Beat egg whites with salt and cream of tartar until stiff but not dry. Fold gently into SPAM mixture. Pile into prepared soufflé dish. Bake in 375°F oven 35 to 40 minutes, or until top is lightly browned and soufflé is set. Serve immediately.

Nice to know: Sauce mixture may be completed ahead of time. Heat sauce and fold in the beaten egg whites just before serving.

Asparagus Roll-Ups

3 Servings

A simple recipe for a sophisticated brunch entrée.

1 package (10 ounces) frozen
asparagus spears
1 can (7 ounces) SPAM, diced
1/4 cup Swiss Cheese Sauce
(below)

12 slices soft white
bread
2 tablespoons butter or
margarine

Cook asparagus according to package directions; drain. Cut asparagus crosswise in 1/2-inch pieces. Combine asparagus, SPAM, and Swiss Cheese Sauce. Remove crusts from bread; flatten by rolling with a rolling pin. Spread butter lightly on one side of each bread slice. Mound some SPAM mixture along one edge of unbuttered side of each bread slice; roll up. Place close together in baking dish, seam side down. Bake in 425°F oven 15 minutes, or until rolls are lightly browned. Serve with additional Swiss Cheese Sauce.

Swiss Cheese Sauce

1 tablespoon butter or
margarine
1 tablespoon all-purpose
flour
1/4 teaspoon salt
1/8 teaspoon paprika

Nutmeg to taste
Pepper to taste
1 cup milk
1 cup shredded Swiss
cheese

In small saucepan, melt butter; blend in flour, salt, paprika, nutmeg, and pepper. Mix in milk; cook over medium heat, stirring until mixture thickens and boils. Add cheese; stir until melted.

Nice to know: You'll have about 1 3/4 cups of sauce left over. Refrigerate and reheat for use another day.

Noontime
Is Anytime

Time to take a break — whether you call it lunch, light supper, or a midnight snack. Relax over meaty Turkey Pita Pockets or a golden, grilled Monte Cristo. Treat your family to delicious Sloppy Josés or Surprise Corned Beef Buns. Rustle up a hot bowl of your own Old-Time Lentil Soup, Minestrone, or Corn Chowder. Come home from school or work to the tantalizing aroma of Home-Style Pizza or Easy Pizza Napoli. And top off a movie or ballgame with Chicken or Tamale Tacos. Take a break anytime — with satisfying sandwiches and soups.

Easy Pizza Napoli   12 Servings

A rich, generous pizza with a different kind of crust.

3 cups biscuit mix	1 can (4 ounces) mushroom
1 1/2 cups beer or water	pieces, drained
1 jar (15 ounces) pizza	1 small onion, thinly
sauce	sliced
2 cups (about 8 ounces)	1 large green pepper,
shredded Cheddar cheese,	seeded and cut
divided	in 12 rings
1 can (12 ounces) SPAM,	1 teaspoon oregano
diced	

In medium bowl, stir together biscuit mix and beer until well mixed. Spread batter over bottom of greased 15×10×1-inch jelly-roll pan. Drizzle sauce over batter; spread carefully to cover surface. Sprinkle with 1/2 the cheese. Top with SPAM, mushrooms, and onion. Arrange green pepper rings over surface to mark 12 separate portions. Sprinkle with remaining cheese and oregano. Bake in 425°F oven 25 to 30 minutes, until crust is golden brown. Let stand 5 minutes before slicing.

Home-Style Pizza   6 Servings

Hungry for a pizza? This one's just about ready to eat!

1 package (13 3/4 ounces)
   hot roll mix
1 cup warm water
1/2 teaspoon oregano
1/4 teaspoon basil
1/8 teaspoon garlic powder
1 can (8 ounces) tomato
   sauce with onions
1 can (7 ounces) SPAM,
   diced

1 small green pepper,
   seeded and cut
   in strips
1 cup (4 ounces) shredded
   mozzarella cheese
1 tablespoon grated
   Parmesan cheese

Combine hot roll mix with water according to package directions for pizza. With greased fingers press dough over greased 14-inch pizza pan, forming a rim around edge of pan. Stir oregano, basil, and garlic powder into tomato sauce; spread over dough. Top with SPAM and green pepper. Sprinkle cheese over top. Bake on rack set low in 425°F oven 20 to 25 minutes, or until edges are golden brown.

Quick Chili Pizza   4 Servings

Quick and nutritious, this snack hits the spot!

1 can (15 ounces) Hormel
   Chili - No Beans
4 English muffins, split
   and lightly toasted

1/4 pound mozzarella or
   other mild cheese,
   sliced
Garlic salt
Oregano

Spoon chili, reserving some, over English muffins. Lay slices of mozzarella over chili. Sprinkle lightly with garlic salt and oregano. Add a dab of chili on top. Broil until cheese melts and pizzas are heated through.

Nice to know: Hormel Chili with Beans can be used to make this pizza extra special.

Turkey Pita Pockets

4 Servings

Take a big, big bite of this overstuffed sandwich — it's absolutely delicious!

1 can (6 3/4 ounces) Hormel
    Chunk Turkey, drained
    and flaked
1 cup bean sprouts
1/2 cup shredded carrot
1/8 teaspoon celery salt
    Dash pepper

1/2 cup plain yogurt,
    divided
4 pita breads (about
    5-inches diameter)
1 cup shredded lettuce
1 tomato, coarsely
    chopped

Combine turkey, sprouts, carrot, celery salt, and pepper; stir in 1/4 cup yogurt. Cut a slit in one third of the outside edge of each pita bread to make a pocket; fill with turkey mixture. Top with lettuce, tomato, and remaining yogurt.

Turkey and Bacon Sandwich

3 Sandwiches

This perfect turkey salad sandwich features bacon and juicy tomato.

1 can (6 3/4 ounces) Hormel
    Chunk Turkey, drained
1/3 cup chopped celery
1/4 cup mayonnaise
1 tablespoon Hormel Bacon
    Bits

6 slices toast
1 medium tomato, thinly
    sliced
    Lettuce leaves

Flake turkey. Mix in celery, mayonnaise, and bacon. Spread mixture on 3 slices toast. Top with tomato slices and lettuce leaves. Cover with remaining toast. Serve immediately.

Hot Meatball Sandwich

3 to 4 Servings

A portable feast for cookouts and camping.

1 can (24 ounces) Dinty
    Moore Meatball Stew

6 to 8 bread slices or
    3 to 4 sandwich buns

Heat stew in saucepan. Toast bread or sandwich buns. With slotted spoon, place meatballs and vegetables on 3 or 4 slices toast or buns. Top with remaining toast or buns; spoon on gravy.

Hero Sandwich

6 Servings

This hero has real Italian flavor!

1 loaf (8 ounces)
  Italian bread
2 tablespoons Italian
  dressing
1 can (12 ounces) SPAM
1 large tomato, thinly
  sliced
1 package (6 ounces)
  sliced Provolone
  cheese

1 jar (7 ounces) roasted
  peppers, drained
1 small red onion,
  thinly sliced
10 pitted black olives,
  halved
  Lettuce leaves

Halve bread lengthwise; scoop out some of center. Drizzle dressing over cut slices of bread. Cut SPAM into 12 slices; overlap 6 slices on bottom of loaf. Top with tomato slices, cheese, peppers, onion, and olives. Overlap remaining SPAM slices over top. Add lettuce leaves. Cover with top half of bread; press down to make a compact package. Wrap in aluminum foil and refrigerate at least 2 hours to blend flavors. Cut crosswise to serve.

VIP Sandwich

1 Serving

A robust bounty of meat and melted cheese.

2 slices bread or 1
  sandwich bun
2 teaspoons butter or
  margarine
2 medium-thick slices SPAM

2 slices tomato
  Bermuda onion, thinly
  sliced
2 slices American cheese

Lightly toast bread or bun; spread with butter. Cover with SPAM; top with tomato. Add onion slices; cover with cheese. Top with remaining toast. Bake in 350°F oven about 10 minutes, or until cheese melts.

Hero Sandwich, Reuben Sandwich (page 30), VIP Sandwich

Reuben Sandwich   4 Sandwiches

A deli classic with an extra-delicious twist.

1 can (8 ounces) sauerkraut
1 cup grated Swiss cheese
1/4 cup Russian dressing
8 slices rye bread

3 tablespoons butter or
   margarine
1 can (12 ounces) SPAM

Rinse sauerkraut; drain well. Combine with cheese and Russian dressing; mix well. Spread each bread slice on one side with butter. Cut SPAM into 8 slices. Spread half of sauerkraut mixture on unbuttered side of 4 bread slices; top each with 2 slices SPAM. Cover with remaining sauerkraut mixture. Top with remaining rye bread, buttered-side up. Grill slowly in skillet or griddle until cheese melts and sandwiches are browned on both sides.

Egg Sandwich Spread   About 2 1/4 Cups

A lunch break that pleases everyone.

1 can (7 ounces) SPAM,
   finely chopped
4 hard-cooked eggs, finely
   chopped
1/4 cup mayonnaise
2 tablespoons chopped celery
2 tablespoons chopped
   green pepper

1 teaspoon minced
   onion
1 teaspoon prepared
   mustard
Pepper to taste

Blend all ingredients. Cover and refrigerate until serving time. Spread on your favorite bread, crackers, or toasted English muffins.

Peppy Sandwich Spread   1 1/4 Cups

A zesty blend for sandwiches or appetizers.

1 can (7 ounces) SPAM
3 slices (2 1/4 ounces)
   American cheese

1 tablespoon pickle relish
1 tablespoon mayonnaise

Finely chop SPAM and cheese or process in food processor using chopping blade. Mix in pickle relish and mayonnaise. Cover and refrigerate until serving time. Serve on bread, toast, pita bread, or crackers.

Monte Cristo Sandwich   6 Sandwiches

*Grilled meat and cheese sandwiched in golden French toast —
it's an all-occasion mealwich!*

1 can (12 ounces) SPAM	2 eggs
6 slices (6 ounces) Muenster cheese, halved	1/4 cup milk
12 slices white bread	3 tablespoons margarine

Cut SPAM into 12 slices. Layer cheese and SPAM on 6 slices
bread; top with remaining bread slices. Mix eggs with
milk; quickly dip both sides of sandwiches into egg
mixture. Sauté in margarine on griddle or skillet over
medium heat until cheese melts and both sides are
browned. Serve immediately.

Cheesy Corned Beef   4 Servings

Toasted cheese tops spiced corned beef for double satisfaction.

4 English muffins, split	2 tablespoons chili sauce
1 can (15 ounces) Mary Kitchen Corned Beef Hash	1/2 teaspoon chili powder
1/4 cup chopped celery	4 slices American cheese
1/4 cup chopped green pepper	

Lightly toast muffins. Combine hash, celery, green
pepper, chili sauce, and chili powder until well mixed.
Pile corned beef mixture on muffin halves. Place on
cookie sheet; bake in 375°F oven 10 minutes. Cut each
cheese slice into 4 triangles; overlap 2 triangles on each
sandwich. Bake 5 minutes longer or until cheese melts.
Serve hot.

Chili Sandwiches   4 Servings

A tomato-topped treasury of chili and cheese.

4 slices bread	1 can (15 ounces) Hormel Chili with Beans
4 tablespoons butter or margarine	4 slices tomato
4 thick slices American cheese	

Butter bread slices; top with a thick slice American
cheese. Place in baking pan; broil until cheese melts and
puffs up. Heat chili; spoon over each sandwich. Top with
tomato slices; broil until tomatoes are hot. Serve immediately.

Grilled Cheese Plus

4 Sandwiches

1 can (12 ounces) SPAM
3 tablespoons butter or
   margarine

8 slices white bread
4 slices American cheese

Cut SPAM into 8 slices. Spread butter on one side of each bread slice. Divide SPAM and cheese onto unbuttered side of 4 bread slices; top with remaining bread slices, buttered side out. Brown on both sides over medium heat on griddle or large skillet. Serve immediately.

Variations:

Layer 2 thin slices tomato with SPAM and cheese.
Add 1 tablespoon pickle relish to each sandwich.
Add layer thinly sliced Bermuda onion with SPAM and cheese.

Open-Face Sandwich Caribe 4 Servings

There's a taste of the tropics in these exciting hot sandwiches.

4 English muffins
   Butter or margarine
   Prepared mustard
1 can (7 ounces) SPAM,
   thinly sliced
8 canned pineapple slices,
   syrup reserved

1 small green pepper,
   seeded and cut
   into 8 rings
1/4 cup firmly-packed
   brown sugar

Lightly toast muffins; spread lightly with butter and mustard. Overlap SPAM slices on each muffin half. Place a pineapple slice and a green pepper ring on each. Combine brown sugar and 4 teaspoons syrup, stirring until smooth; spoon over sandwiches. Place on cookie sheet; bake in 375°F oven 10 minutes. Serve hot.

Chicken Tacos

8 Servings

Superbly seasoned chicken makes tacos terrific!

1 can (8 ounces) tomato sauce	1 can (6 3/4 ounces) Hormel Chunk Chicken
1 teaspoon chili powder	8 taco shells
1/2 teaspoon cumin	3/4 cup (about 3 1/2 ounces) shredded Monterey Jack cheese
1/4 teaspoon oregano	
1 small clove garlic, minced	
1/3 cup chopped onion	1 1/2 cups finely-shredded lettuce
1 tablespoon cooking oil	

In small saucepan, combine tomato sauce, chili powder, cumin, oregano, and garlic. Heat to boiling, stirring occasionally; reserve. In medium skillet, sauté onion in oil until golden. Drain chicken reserving broth. Flake chicken; add with broth to skillet. Mix in 1/3 cup tomato sauce. Simmer 5 minutes until slightly thickened. To serve, partially fill taco shells with chicken mixture. Sprinkle with cheese; top with lettuce. Serve with remaining heated tomato sauce.

Hash and Chili Tacos

8 to 10 Servings

Teen-agers can prepare these tacos for their next party.

1 can (15 ounces) Mary Kitchen Roast Beef Hash	8 to 10 taco shells
	Diced tomato
1 can (15 ounces) Hormel Chili - No Beans	Shredded Cheddar cheese
	Shredded lettuce
1/2 cup chopped green pepper	

In medium saucepan, combine hash, chili, and green pepper; cook and stir until hot. Spoon into taco shells and garnish with tomato, cheese, and lettuce.

Microwave directions: In 1 1/2-quart baking dish combine hash, chili, and green pepper; stir to mix well. Cover and microwave 3 minutes. Stir and microwave, covered, 3 minutes more. Let stand 5 minutes. Spoon into taco shells and garnish as above.

Surprise Corned Beef Buns   6 Servings

You'll savor the surprise sealed inside these juicy corned beef patties.

3 slices American cheese
2 cans (15 ounces each) Mary Kitchen Corned Beef Hash, divided

12 cucumber pickle slices
6 hamburger buns, split

Quarter cheese slices; reserve. Spoon hash from one can to make 6 mounds on baking sheet; flatten in patties the size of hamburger buns. Top each patty with 2 cheese quarters and 2 pickle slices. Top with remaining can of hash making sure to completely enclose cheese and pickle. Bake in 425°F oven 15 minutes. Toast split buns in oven for last 5 minutes baking time. Place patties between toasted buns.

Sloppy José   3 or 4 Servings

Try this marvelous Mexican version of the classic Sloppy Joe.

1/2 cup chopped celery
1/4 cup chopped green pepper
       Butter or margarine
1 can (15 ounces) Hormel Tamales
1 can (15 ounces) Hormel Chili - No Beans (or with Beans)

1 loaf (8 ounces) Italian bread
    Shredded Cheddar cheese
    Sliced green onions

Sauté celery and green pepper in 2 tablespoons butter until tender. Remove papers from tamales; slice tamales into bite-size pieces. In medium saucepan, combine tamales, chili, celery, and green pepper; cook until hot, stirring occasionally. Halve bread lengthwise, then cut into sections; spread with butter and toast lightly. Place bread, cut side up, on ovenproof serving plates or on a baking sheet. Spoon chili mixture over bread; sprinkle with cheese. Broil until cheese melts. Garnish with green onions.

Nice to know: You can substitute sandwich buns, corn bread, or toast for the Italian bread.

Hearty Tacos
8 Servings

Olé for true Mexican flavor!

1 can (16 ounces) refried
  beans
1 can (7 ounces) SPAM,
  chopped
2 tablespoons taco sauce,
  mild or hot

8 taco shells
  Shredded Monterey Jack
    cheese
  Shredded lettuce
  Chopped tomato

In medium bowl, combine refried beans, SPAM, and taco sauce stirring until well mixed. Spoon into taco shells. Place filled shells in baking dish; cover and bake in 400°F oven about 15 minutes or until warm. Serve with cheese, lettuce, tomato and extra taco sauce.

Nice to know: Guacamole or diced avocado also make great toppings for tacos.

Tamale Tacos
8 Servings

A triple treat for Mexican-food fans.

1 can (15 ounces) Hormel
  Tamales
1 can (15 ounces) Hormel
  Chili - No Beans
8 taco shells

Shredded Cheddar cheese
Chopped tomatoes
Shredded lettuce
Dairy sour cream

Remove papers from tamales; heat through in small saucepan. Heat chili in another saucepan. Warm taco shells in oven. Carefully place 1 heated tamale in the fold of each shell. Top with 1/4 cup chili. Garnish with cheese, tomatoes, and lettuce to taste. Top with a dollop of sour cream.

Mulligan Soup

2 Servings

If you like Mulligan Stew, you'll love this soup.

> 1 can (7 1/2 ounces) Dinty
>   Moore Brunswick Stew
> 1 can (8 ounces) stewed
>   tomatoes
> 1/3 cup water

In small saucepan, combine all ingredients; bring to a boil. Simmer 2 minutes, stirring once or twice, and serve.

Old-Time Lentil Soup

2 1/2 Quarts

A thick, delicious winter warm-up.

> 1 pound lentils
> 2 large ribs celery with
>   tops, cut in thirds
> 1 large carrot, scraped and
>   halved
> 1 medium onion, coarsely
>   chopped
> 1 teaspoon minced garlic

> 1 teaspoon salt
> 1/8 teaspoon pepper
> 2 quarts water
> 1 can (7 ounces) SPAM,
>   cubed
> 1 tablespoon white
>   vinegar

In large pot, combine lentils, celery, carrot, onion, garlic, salt, pepper, and water; bring to a boil. Cover and simmer 45 minutes. Remove from heat; cool slightly. Place half of lentils and all celery and carrot in food processor or blender; process until puréed. Return to pot. Add SPAM to soup. Bring to a boil; cover and simmer 15 minutes. Stir in vinegar. Mix well before ladling into soup bowls.

Corn Chowder

1 1/2 Quarts

Ready whenever you are — for lunch, dinner, or an impromptu party.

1/2 cup chopped onion
1/2 cup chopped green pepper
1 tablespoon butter or
   margarine
2 cans (1 pound each) cream-
   style corn

2 cups milk
1 can (7 ounces) SPAM,
   diced
1/4 teaspoon garlic salt
Pepper to taste

In medium saucepan, sauté onion and green pepper in butter until vegetables are tender but not browned. Add corn, milk, SPAM, garlic salt, and pepper; bring to a boil over medium heat stirring often. Lower heat; cover and simmer 10 minutes.

Split Pea and Ham Soup

2 Quarts

This rich soup served with French bread or toast makes a hearty one-pot meal.

1 cup (1/2 pound) split
   green peas
1 cup peeled and diced
   potatoes
1/2 cup diced carrots
1/2 cup chopped celery
1 medium onion, chopped

6 cups water
1 1/2 teaspoons salt, divided
1/4 teaspoon pepper
1 can (6 3/4 ounces)
   Hormel Chunk Ham
1 large clove garlic

In large saucepan, combine split peas, potatoes, carrots, celery, onion, water, 1/2 teaspoon salt, and pepper. Drain liquid from ham into saucepan. Coarsely chop ham; add to saucepan. Bring to boil; cover and simmer 1 hour. Crush garlic with remaining 1 teaspoon salt; stir into soup. Cover and simmer 30 minutes longer.

Mulligatawny Soup

5 Cups

A delicate dinner prelude — chicken soup enticingly spiced.

1/3 cup chopped onion
1/4 cup chopped carrot
1/4 cup chopped celery
3 tablespoons butter or margarine
2 tablespoons flour
1 tablespoon curry powder

2 cans (13 3/4 ounces each) chicken broth
1 can (6 3/4 ounces) Hormel Chunk Chicken, drained and flaked
1 cup light cream

In medium saucepan, sauté onion, carrot, and celery in butter until onion is transparent. Blend in flour and curry powder until smooth; stir in chicken broth. Cook over medium heat, stirring until mixture thickens and boils. Lower heat; cover and simmer 10 minutes. Add chicken and cream; heat and serve.

Microwave directions: In 2 1/2-quart casserole, combine onion, carrot, celery, and butter. Microwave 3 minutes. Stir in flour and curry powder until smooth; mix in broth. Cover and microwave 4 minutes. Stir; cover and microwave 4 minutes more. Mix in remaining ingredients; cover and microwave 2 minutes. Let stand 5 minutes.

Potato and Bacon Soup

2 Servings

A creamy potato soup with the smoky taste of bacon.

1 can (7 1/2 ounces) Hormel Au Gratin Potatoes 'n Bacon
1 can water

1/2 cup instant nonfat dry milk
Salt and pepper to taste

In small saucepan, combine Au Gratin Potatoes 'n Bacon, water, and dry milk. Cook and stir over medium heat until mixture comes to a boil. Simmer 2 minutes. Season with salt and pepper.

Extra Noodles Chicken Soup 4 Servings

Extra fun around a campfire, extra energy for a cold-weather lunch.

>   1 envelope noodle soup mix
>   2 cans (7 1/2 ounces each)
>   Dinty Moore Noodles
>   and Chicken

Prepare soup mix according to package directions. Stir in Noodles and Chicken; heat to serving temperature.

Minestrone Soup 3 1/2 Quarts

Simmer a garden of goodness in this satisfying soup supper.

>   1 can (12 ounces) SPAM,
>   finely chopped
>   1 medium onion, finely
>   chopped
>   1 rib celery, finely
>   chopped
>   1 medium carrot, finely
>   chopped
>   2 cloves garlic, minced
>   2 tablespoons cooking oil
>   2 quarts water
> 1/2 teaspoon basil
>   1 bay leaf
>   3 cups (3/4 pound)
>   chopped cabbage

>   2 medium potatoes, peeled
>   and diced
>   2 medium tomatoes,
>   peeled and chopped
>   1 medium zucchini, diced
>   1 small white turnip,
>   diced
> 1/2 teaspoon salt
>   1 can (16 ounces) pinto
>   beans, undrained
> 1/4 cup long-grain rice
>   Parmesan cheese

In large pot, sauté SPAM, onion, celery, carrot, and garlic in oil until lightly browned, stirring often. Add water, basil, and bay leaf; bring to a boil. Cover and simmer 10 minutes. Add cabbage, potatoes, tomatoes, zucchini, turnip, and salt. Cover and gently boil 15 minutes. Add pinto beans and rice; cover and cook 15 minutes longer. Serve in large soup bowls with a sprinkling of grated Parmesan cheese, if desired.

Potato Chowder   1 1/2 Quarts

A hot savory chill-chaser loaded with chunks of meat and potatoes.

1 medium onion, chopped
1/2 cup chopped celery
1 tablespoon butter or
    margarine
1 can (7 ounces) SPAM,
    diced
1 can (10 3/4 ounces)
    condensed chicken broth

1 cup water
1 pound potatoes, peeled
    and diced (about 3
    medium)
1/2 teaspoon caraway seeds
    Pepper to taste
1 1/2 cups half-and-half
1/4 cup chopped parsley

In medium saucepan, sauté onion and celery in butter until tender. Add SPAM; cook 3 minutes, stirring often. Add chicken broth, water, potatoes, caraway, and pepper. Cover and cook until potatoes are tender, about 10 minutes. Stir in half-and-half and parsley; heat and serve.

Serve Them Hot, Serve Them Cold

Crisp abundance, bright colors — salads hit the spot! Dress them with imagination, season them with surprises and you've got the perfect answers for warm-weather dining, elegant luncheons, and well-balanced everyday menus. Pick Spinach Salad from the garden, Hot Potato Salad from the winter pantry, and Canteloupe Salad from summer's ripe harvest. Serve Chicken-Grape Salad, Curried Turkey-Avocado Salad, or Riviera Salad for refreshment outdoors. Or warm up a meal spectacularly with Hot Chef's Salad and Hot Spiced Fruit. From updated Caesar and Waldorf salads to creative Antipasto and Aloha salads, there's enough bounty here to tempt every taste!

Curried Turkey-Avocado Salad

4 Servings

Melon spices and the crunch of almonds heighten the luxury of a rich salad served in avocado shells.

- 2 ripe avocados (about 3/4 pound each)
- 1 can (6 3/4 ounces) Hormel Chunk Turkey, drained and flaked
- 1/2 cup thinly-sliced celery
- 3 tablespoons lemon juice
- 1 tablespoon honey
- 1 tablespoon chopped chutney
- 1/2 teaspoon curry powder
- 1/4 teaspoon garlic salt
- Pepper to taste
- Slivered almonds

Halve and pit avocados. Carefully scoop out flesh leaving shells intact. Coarsely chop avocado; combine with turkey and celery. Mix remaining ingredients except almonds; pour over avocado mixture. Stir gently to mix well. Pile back into shells; sprinkle with almonds.

Chicken-Grape Salad

4 Servings

The best of everything — chicken, green grapes, and almonds in a glorious creamy salad.

1 can (6 3/4 ounces) Hormel
   Chunk Chicken, drained
   and flaked
1 cup seedless grapes
1/3 cup chopped celery
1/4 cup chopped green pepper
2 tablespoons slivered
   almonds

1/4 cup mayonnaise
2 tablespoons dairy
   sour cream
1 teaspoon lemon juice
1/4 teaspoon salt
   Pepper to taste
   Lettuce leaves
1 tomato, cut in wedges

Combine chicken with grapes, celery, green pepper, and almonds. Mix mayonnaise, sour cream, lemon juice, salt and pepper. Just before serving, toss dressing with chicken mixture. Mound chicken salad on lettuce leaves; add tomato wedges.

BLT Salad

4 Servings

Clever calorie-counting! The taste of a favorite sandwich in a streamlined salad.

1/3 cup plain yogurt
2 teaspoons cooking oil
1/8 teaspoon sugar
   Dash dry mustard
   Pepper to taste

2 tablespoons Hormel
   Bacon Bits
2 large tomatoes, sliced
   (about 1 pound)
4 lettuce leaves

Combine yogurt, oil, sugar, mustard, and pepper; stir to mix well. Just before serving stir in bacon. Arrange tomato slices on lettuce leaves; pour dressing over. Sprinkle with additional bacon.

Chicken-Grape Salad, BLT Salad

Antipasto Salad

6 Servings

What to serve with spaghetti, lasagna, and other Italian fare? Here's the perfect answer.

1 can (16 ounces) chick peas, drained
1 small green pepper, seeded and chopped
1 small red onion, thinly sliced
1 can (2 1/2 ounces) pitted black olives, drained
1/2 cup Italian dressing

4 cups torn romaine
2 cups torn lettuce
1 can (12 ounces) SPAM, diced
4 ounces Provolone cheese, cubed
2 tomatoes, each cut into 6 wedges

In small bowl, combine chick peas, green pepper, onion, olives, and dressing. Cover and refrigerate at least 1 hour. Just before serving, combine romaine and lettuce in salad bowl; pour on chick pea mixture. Top with SPAM, cheese, and tomatoes. Toss gently to mix well. Serve immediately.

Turkey Salad Juarez

3 Servings

A hearty, all-seasons main course salad.

2 cups cooked rice
1 can (6 1/2 ounces) Hormel Chunk Turkey, drained and flaked
2/3 cup cooked whole-kernel corn
1/2 cup thinly-sliced celery
1/3 cup mayonnaise

1 tablespoon finely-chopped canned green chilies
1/2 teaspoon salt
1/4 teaspoon chili powder
Lettuce leaves
2 medium tomatoes, peeled and cut into 6 wedges each

Combine rice, turkey, corn, and celery. Combine mayonnaise, chilies, salt, and chili powder; mix into turkey mixture. Place lettuce leaves on 3 plates; mound salad in center. Arrange 4 tomato wedges on each plate.

Note: To peel tomatoes, plunge into boiling water for 2 minutes. Remove from water; peel off skin.

Wilted Lettuce Salad

6 to 8 Servings

A hot tossed salad enriched with bacon and chopped eggs.

1/2 cup cooking oil
1/4 cup vinegar
  2 quarts torn lettuce
  4 tablespoons Hormel
       Bacon Bits

1 cup red onion rings
2 hard-cooked eggs,
     chopped

Heat oil and vinegar over low heat, stirring occasionally. Combine lettuce, bacon, and onions. Add hot dressing; toss lightly. Top with eggs.

Spinach Salad

6 Servings

1/4 cup cooking oil
  2 tablespoons red wine
       vinegar
  2 tablespoons finely-
       chopped onion
1/4 teaspoon pepper

1 1/2 quarts torn spinach
    2 tablespoons Hormel
         Bacon Bits
    1 hard-cooked egg,
         chopped

Heat oil, vinegar, onion, and pepper over low heat, stirring occasionally. Combine spinach and bacon. Add hot dressing; toss lightly. Top with egg.

Marinated Bean Salad

4 Servings

Cool and refreshing, yet full of satisfaction.

1 can (16 ounces) pink beans,
     drained and rinsed
1 can (7 ounces) SPAM, diced
1/2 cup chopped celery
1/4 cup chopped green pepper
1 tablespoon finely-chopped
     onion

1/4 teaspoon garlic salt
     Dash pepper
  1 medium tomato,
       coarsely chopped
1/4 cup Italian dressing
     Lettuce leaves

Combine beans, SPAM, celery, green pepper, onion, garlic salt, and pepper. Cover and refrigerate until chilled. Just before serving, gently stir in tomato. Pour dressing over all; mix gently but well. Pile mixture on lettuce-lined serving plates.

Hot Chicken Salad

4 to 6 Servings

A wonderful casserole for covered suppers and party buffets.

2 cans (6 3/4 ounces) Hormel
  Chunk Chicken
1 cup celery slices
1/2 cup coleslaw dressing
1/4 cup green onion slices
2 tablespoons chopped
  pimientos

1 teaspoon salt
1/8 teaspoon pepper
1 cup (4 ounces) shredded
  Swiss cheese
1 tablespoon flour

Combine chicken, celery, dressing, onion, pimientos, and seasonings; mix well. Toss cheese with flour. Add to chicken mixture; mix lightly. Spoon into 1-quart casserole. Bake in 350°F oven, 30 minutes.

Waldorf Salad

4 Servings

A classic, its crispness enhanced with diced meat and chopped pecans.

2 apples, cored and diced
1 tablespoon lemon juice
1 can (7 ounces) SPAM, diced
1 cup thinly sliced celery
1/3 cup raisins

1/2 cup mayonnaise
  Lettuce leaves
2 tablespoons chopped
  pecans

Sprinkle apples with lemon juice. Toss apples with SPAM, celery, and raisins. Add mayonnaise; mix gently but well. Pile onto lettuce-lined serving plates; sprinkle with pecans. Serve immediately.

Nice to know: You can omit the raisins and serve with toasted raisin bread if you prefer.

Hot Spiced Fruit

4 to 6 Servings

The fragrance of spiced fruit complements roasts, chops, or ham.

1 can (16 ounces) peach
  halves, drained
1 can (16 ounces) pear
  halves, undrained
1/2 cup Russian dressing

1 teaspoon whole cloves
1 teaspoon cinnamon
1 tablespoon Hormel
  Bacon Bits

Combine all ingredients except bacon in saucepan. Simmer 15 minutes, stirring occasionally. Sprinkle with bacon. Serve immediately.

Potato Salad

2 Quarts

Luscious potato salad becomes the main attraction when you add meat and vegetables.

2 pounds potatoes (6 medium)
1 can (12 ounces) SPAM, cubed
1/2 cup cooked diced carrots
1/2 cup frozen peas, thawed
1/2 cup chopped dill pickles

1/4 cup finely-chopped onion
3/4 cup mayonnaise
2 tablespoons dill pickle liquid
Salt and pepper to taste

Cook unpeeled potatoes in boiling salted water until tender; drain. Cool slightly; peel. Cool to room temperature; cut into 1/2-inch cubes. Combine SPAM with potatoes in large bowl. Gently mix in carrots, peas, pickles, and onion. Stir together mayonnaise and pickle liquid; gently stir into SPAM mixture. Season to taste with salt and pepper. Cover and refrigerate until serving time, at least 1 hour.

Aloha Salad

6 Servings

A rice ring filled with bright pineapple-ham salad. Call it Hawaiian eye-appeal!

1 cup long-grain rice
1 can (20 ounces) pineapple chunks
2 cans (6 3/4 ounces each) Hormel Chunk Ham, drained and coarsely chopped
2/3 cup thinly-sliced celery

1/3 cup chopped green pepper
2/3 cup mayonnaise
2 tablespoons honey
1 tablespoon lemon juice
1/8 teaspoon ground ginger
Lettuce leaves

Cook rice according to package directions. Cool slightly; pack into well-oiled 4-cup ring mold. Cool to room temperature; chill. Drain pineapple reserving 1 tablespoon syrup. Combine ham, pineapple chunks, celery, and green pepper; chill. Before serving, mix mayonnaise, honey, lemon juice, ginger, and reserved tablespoon pineapple syrup. Pour 1/2 cup dressing over ham mixture; mix gently. Unmold rice onto lettuce-lined serving plate. Spoon ham mixture into center of ring. Serve with remaining dressing.

Nice to know: You get the benefit of added protein by using the juice in Hormel Chunk Ham. Combine juice with ham.

Pineapple Petal Salad

2 Servings

The pleasures of a salad that looks as lovely as it tastes.

1 can (6 3/4 ounces) Hormel
    Chunk Ham, flaked
1/4 cup chopped green pepper
2 tablespoons chopped celery
2 teaspoons chopped stuffed
    green olives

1/4 cup mayonnaise
    Lettuce leaves
4 canned pineapple
    slices, drained and
    chilled

Combine ham, green pepper, celery, olives, and mayonnaise. Cover and chill until serving time. Arrange lettuce leaves on 2 salad plates. Halve pineapple slices; place 4 halves on each plate to form a scalloped edge. Mound ham mixture in center. Garnish with additional olive, if desired.

Riviera Salad

4 Servings

Complete convenience: a do-ahead supper salad ready for last-minute tossing.

6 tablespoons cooking oil
2 tablespoons vinegar
1 teaspoon prepared
    mustard
1/2 teaspoon thyme
1/4 teaspoon salt
1/8 teaspoon pepper
1 clove garlic, minced
1 pound potatoes (3 medium)
1/2 pound fresh green
    beans

1 small red onion,
    thinly sliced
1 quart bite-size
    lettuce pieces
1 can (12 ounces) SPAM,
    cubed
1 can (3 1/2 ounces)
    pitted black olives,
    drained

Combine cooking oil, vinegar, mustard, thyme, salt, pepper, and garlic; mix well; reserve. Cook unpeeled potatoes until tender; drain. Cool to room temperature; peel and cube. Cut beans into 1-inch lengths; cook until tender crisp; drain and cool to room temperature. Combine potatoes, green beans, and onion; cover and refrigerate until cold. Before serving, place lettuce in salad bowl; top with vegetable mixture. Pile SPAM in center; sprinkle olives over top. Pour on reserved dressing; toss well.

Avocado Mousse Salad

8 Servings

Creamy avocados seasoned with intrigue and served with a touch of sophistication.

2 large ripe avocados (about 3/4 pound each)
1 can (7 ounces) SPAM, cut in chunks
Juice of 1 lemon
1/2 cup dairy sour cream
1/4 teaspoon salt

Few drops hot pepper sauce
1 envelope unflavored gelatin
1/4 cup cold water
Lettuce leaves
Pitted black olives

Halve, pit, and peel avocados; cut into chunks. Combine avocado, SPAM, lemon juice, sour cream, salt, and pepper sauce in food processor or blender and process until smooth. Soften gelatin in cold water; dissolve over boiling water. Stir in avocado mixture. Divide into eight 1/2-cup molds. Refrigerate at least 2 hours. To serve unmold onto lettuce-lined salad plates; garnish with black olives, if desired.

Nice to know: You can make this salad in individual molds or in one 4-cup mold.

Cantaloupe Salad

4 Servings

A sublime summer cooler, with refreshing pineapple yogurt dressing.

Lettuce leaves
1 can (12 ounces) SPAM, cut in chunks
1 medium cantaloupe, seeded, peeled, and cut in chunks
1 small green pepper, seeded and chopped

1 can (8 ounces) crushed pineapple, drained
3 tablespoons dairy sour cream
3 tablespoons yogurt
1/4 teaspoon sugar

Place lettuce leaves on salad plates; mound SPAM in center. Surround with cantaloupe. Sprinkle green pepper over top. Combine pineapple, sour cream, yogurt, and sugar; pour over salad.

Festive Salad

6 Servings

Arrange this salad in a clear glass bowl to show off its festive red and white layers.

2 pounds potatoes
(6 medium)
1/3 cup mayonnaise
1/3 cup dairy sour cream
1/2 cup chopped celery
1/3 cup chopped onion
1/4 cup chopped green pepper
1 tablespoon milk
1/2 teaspoon salt

Pepper to taste
1 can (12 ounces) SPAM,
diced, divided
1 cup halved cherry
tomatoes
Green pepper rings
Radishes, coarsely
chopped

Cook potatoes in boiling salted water until tender; drain. Cool slightly; peel. When cooled to room temperature, slice thin. In medium bowl, combine mayonnaise, sour cream, celery, onion, green pepper, milk, salt, and pepper; gently stir in potatoes. In 2-quart serving dish, spread one quarter of the potato salad over bottom; sprinkle with half of SPAM. Add another one quarter of the potato salad, then cherry tomatoes. Finish with 2 more layers of potato salad separated by remaining SPAM. Cover and refrigerate at least 2 hours to blend flavors. Before serving, garnish with green pepper rings and chopped radishes.

Stuffed Tomatoes

4 Servings

Cut tomatoes into "flower" holders for ham and rice salad.

1 can (7 ounces) Hormel
Chunk Ham, flaked
1 cup cold cooked rice
1/2 cup frozen peas, thawed
1/4 cup chopped celery

1/3 cup mayonnaise
Dash pepper
4 small tomatoes
Lettuce leaves
Pitted black olives

In small bowl, combine ham, rice, peas, celery, mayonnaise, and pepper. Remove stem end of tomatoes; slit each tomato into 6 wedges but do not cut through completely to bottom. Spread out wedges; place on lettuce-lined plates. Mound ham salad in center; top each with a pitted black olive.

Festive Salad, Baked Ham (page 65) with Cherry Jubilee Sauce (page 66)

Salad-Stuffed Peppers

4 Servings

For luncheon on the patio or a light summer supper, serve peppers filled with a colorful mélange.

4 green peppers, halved and
  seeded
1 can (7 ounces) SPAM, diced
1 can (8 3/4 ounces) whole-
  kernel corn, drained
1/2 cup chopped celery
1/4 cup shredded Monterey
  Jack cheese

1 tablespoon minced
  onion
Dash pepper
3 tablespoons Italian
  dressing
3 cups shredded lettuce
1 can pimientos, cut
  into strips

Simmer pepper halves in boiling water 2 minutes, making sure peppers are completely covered. Drain and rinse with cold water; refrigerate until cold. Combine SPAM, corn, celery, cheese, onion, and pepper; mix with dressing. Spoon onto pepper halves. Divide lettuce into 4 salad plates; place 2 filled peppers on each plate. Garnish tops with pimiento strips.

Hot Potato Salad

6 Servings

Just the right balance of seasonings and spices ensures tantalizing Old World flavor.

2 1/2 pounds potatoes
1/2 cup sliced radishes
1/2 cup chopped parsley
1/4 cup Hormel Bacon Bits
3/4 teaspoon celery seed
1/2 cup chopped onions
2 tablespoons cooking oil

1 tablespoon flour
3/4 teaspoon salt
1/8 teaspoon pepper
1/2 cup water
3/4 cup vinegar
2 tablespoons sugar

Cook unpeeled potatoes in small amount boiling salted water until tender; drain. Cool slightly; peel. Dice potatoes; combine with radishes, parsley, bacon, and celery seed. In small saucepan, sauté onions in oil until transparent; blend in flour, salt, and pepper. Add water, vinegar, and sugar; cook over medium heat, stirring until mixture thickens and boils. Pour hot sauce over potato mixture; stir gently to mix well. Serve warm.

Mousse Salad

6 Servings

A delicately flavored ring mold to frame crudités or cooked vegetables.

1 can (13 3/4 ounces) chicken
   broth, divided
1 envelope unflavored
   gelatin
1 tablespoon minced onion

1 can (12 ounces) SPAM,
   finely chopped
1/2 cup finely-chopped
   celery
1 cup dairy sour cream

In small saucepan, stir together 1 cup broth, gelatin, and onion; cook over low heat, stirring until mixture simmers. Cook slightly. In mixing bowl, combine SPAM with gelatin mixture, remaining broth, celery, and sour cream. Pour into 4- or 5-cup ring mold. Chill at least 4 hours. Just before serving, invert onto serving plate and fill center of mold as desired.

Nice to know: For a spectacular presentation, fill the ring with marinated, barely-cooked mixed vegetables.

Three Bean Salad

6 Servings

Bean salad a little bit different — great for potluck parties and suppers!

1 can (7 ounces) SPAM, diced
1 can (16 ounces) cut green
   beans, drained
1 can (16 ounces) yellow
   wax beans, drained
1 can (16 ounces) cannellini,
   drained (white kidney
   beans)

1/3 cup finely-chopped
   onion
1/3 cup cooking oil
1/3 cup cider vinegar
1/3 cup sugar
1/4 teaspoon salt
1/8 teaspoon pepper

In medium bowl, combine SPAM, green beans, wax beans, cannellini, and onion. Combine remaining ingredients; pour over SPAM mixture. Stir gently, mixing thoroughly. Cover and refrigerate at least 3 hours before serving, stirring several times.

Rosy Ham Mold

4 Cups

2 cans (6 3/4 ounces each)
  Hormel Chunk Ham
1 envelope unflavored
  gelatin
1 can (10 3/4 ounces)
  condensed tomato soup
1 cup mayonnaise

1/2 cup finely-chopped
  celery
2 tablespoons minced
  onion
1 tablespoon prepared
  horseradish

Drain ham, reserving juices. Add water to juices, if necessary, to make 1/4 cup; stir in gelatin. Dissolve gelatin over boiling water; set aside. Finely chop ham; mix in soup, mayonnaise, celery, onion, and horseradish. Stir in gelatin. Pour into 1-quart mold; cover and refrigerate at least 3 hours. Just before serving, unmold onto serving plate. Serve with crackers.

Chicken Mousse Mold

4 Cups

Sure to disappear quickly, this superb chicken spread is perfect for a luncheon or predinner nibbling.

2 cans (6 3/4 ounces each)
  Hormel Chunk Chicken
1 envelope unflavored gelatin
1 can (10 3/4 ounces)
  condensed cream of
  mushroom soup

1 cup dairy sour cream
2/3 cup finely-chopped
  celery
1/4 teaspoon onion powder

Drain chicken, reserving broth. Soften gelatin in broth; dissolve over boiling water; set aside. Finely chop chicken; mix in soup, sour cream, celery, and onion powder. Stir in gelatin. Pour into 1-quart mold; cover and refrigerate at least 3 hours. Just before serving, unmold onto serving plate. Circle with crackers or melba toast.

Macaroni Salad
2 Quarts

An unusual tangy dressing for an ever-popular side dish.

1/2 pound elbow macaroni	1/2 cup dairy sour cream
1 can (12 ounces) SPAM, chopped	1/2 cup plain yogurt
2/3 cup sliced celery	2 teaspoons prepared mustard
1/2 cup sliced green onions	Salt and pepper to taste
1/4 cup sweet pickle relish, drained	

Cook elbow macaroni according to package directions. Drain and rinse with cold water. In large bowl, combine macaroni, SPAM, celery, onions, and pickle relish. Stir together sour cream, yogurt, and mustard until well blended. Gently mix into macaroni-SPAM mixture. Season to taste with salt and pepper. Cover and refrigerate at least 3 hours to blend flavors.

Chef's Salad
4 Servings

Keep these ingredients on hand for busy days and unexpected guests.

1 quart torn salad greens	1 can (6 3/4 ounces) Hormel Chunk Turkey, drained and flaked
1 tomato, coarsely chopped	
1 can (6 3/4 ounces) Hormel Chunk Ham, drained and flaked	1 hard-cooked egg, sliced
2 ounces Swiss cheese, cut in thin strips	1/4 cup pitted black olives, halved
	1/3 cup Italian dressing

Place greens in shallow salad bowl. Sprinkle tomato around edges of bowl. Add a circle of ham, then a circle of cheese. Fill center with turkey. Top with egg slices; sprinkle olives over all. Just before serving, toss well with dressing.

Caesar Salad

4 Servings

A splendid salad for an elegant dinner party.

1 1/2 quarts torn salad greens
  1/2 cup croutons
    2 tablespoons Hormel
       Bacon Bits
    1 tablespoon grated Parmesan
       cheese
    3 tablespoons cooking oil

1 tablespoon lemon juice
1/2 teaspoon Worcester-
    shire sauce
1/4 teaspoon garlic salt
    Dash pepper
1 egg

Combine greens, croutons, bacon, and cheese in salad bowl. Combine oil, lemon juice, Worcestershire, garlic salt, and pepper until well blended. Break egg over salad; pour dressing over all. Toss gently but well until all ingredients are coated with dressing.

Hot Chef's Salad

4 to 6 Servings

Heating enhances the flavor of a bountiful chef's salad.

1/2 cup Italian dressing
1/2 tablespoon sugar
  1 can (7 ounces) SPAM, cut
    in strips
  1 can (6 3/4 ounces) Hormel
    Chunk Chicken, drained
    and flaked
  2 hard-cooked eggs, sliced

1/4 cup sliced celery
  2 cups lettuce, torn
    into bite-size pieces
3/4 cup julienne-style
    Swiss cheese strips
  1 small tomato, cut
    into thin wedges

In large skillet, combine dressing and sugar; heat to boiling. Layer SPAM, chicken, eggs, celery, lettuce, cheese, and tomato in hot dressing; cover and cook over medium heat 5 minutes. Toss and serve immediately.

The Family's Favorites

There's something wonderful simmering in the kitchen. . . . Is it Stuffed Cabbage, or Baked Ham with Apple Cider Sauce? Or is it something a little bit different — like Cantonese Sweet and Sour, Linguini Milano, or Heidelberg Casserole? Whatever it is, it smells delicious! Hearty main courses, casseroles, and side dishes bring the whole family together — for who could resist Reuben Baked Potatoes, Confetti Hash Peppers, or sausage-topped Baked Turkey Loaf!

Blanka's Pork Patties   4 Servings

Blanka's family enjoys these patties as much today as she did as a child in Czechoslovakia.

3/4 pound (1/2 medium head) curly cabbage	3/4 cup dry bread crumbs, divided
1 can (12 ounces) SPAM	1/8 teaspoon pepper
1 medium onion	1 tablespoon water
2 cloves garlic	Cooking oil
2 eggs, divided	

Cut cabbage into wedges; remove core. Cook in small amount salted boiling water until tender; drain well. Finely chop cabbage or process in food processor using chopping blade. Transfer to medium bowl. Finely chop SPAM, onion, and garlic or process in food processor. Mix into cabbage with 1 egg, 1/4 cup bread crumbs, and pepper. Shape mixture into 8 balls; flatten to make patties about 1/2-inch thick. Beat remaining egg with water. Dip patties first in egg-water mixture, then in remaining bread crumbs to coat both sides. Sauté in 1/4-inch oil over medium heat until browned on both sides.

SPAM Divan Bake

4 Servings

Count on this combination for enduring popularity.

1 small bunch broccoli (about 1 pound)	Dash cayenne
3 tablespoons butter or margarine	1 1/2 cups milk
3 tablespoons flour	4 slices (4 ounces) American cheese, cut in small pieces
1/2 teaspoon onion powder	1 can (12 ounces) SPAM
1/4 teaspoon dry mustard	Paprika
1/2 teaspoon salt	

Remove outer leaves and tough part of broccoli stalks; separate into smaller lengthwise pieces. Cook in small amount of boiling salted water until tender; drain. Melt butter in medium saucepan; blend in flour, onion powder, mustard, salt, and cayenne. Stir in milk. Cook over medium heat, stirring until mixture thickens and boils. Add cheese; cook, stirring until cheese melts. Arrange broccoli in a single layer in buttered 12×8-inch baking dish; pour about half of sauce over broccoli. Cut SPAM into 8 slices; overlap slices on top. Pour remaining sauce over top; sprinkle with paprika. Bake in 425°F oven 10 minutes, or until piping hot.

SPAM à la King

4 Servings

A la breakfast, à la dinner – à la king supreme.

1/3 cup chopped green pepper	1 chicken flavor bouillon cube
3 tablespoons butter or margarine	1 can (12 ounces) SPAM, cubed
3 tablespoons flour	1 can (4 ounces) mushrooms, drained
1/4 teaspoon salt	1/4 cup chopped canned pimiento
Pepper to taste	
1 cup water	
1 cup half-and-half	

In large saucepan, sauté green pepper in butter until tender. Blend in flour, salt, and pepper until smooth. Stir in water, half-and-half, and bouillon; cook over low heat, stirring until bouillon dissolves and mixture boils and thickens. Add SPAM, mushrooms, and pimiento; cook and stir 3 minutes. Serve over rice or toast.

Baked Turkey Loaf

4 to 6 Servings

A double attraction — sausages and turkey baked in a handsome loaf.

1 can (5 ounces) Hormel Chicken Vienna Sausages	1/4 cup dry bread crumbs
1 pound ground raw turkey	1 egg
1/2 pound carrots, grated	1/3 cup dairy sour cream
1 small onion, chopped	3/4 teaspoon salt
3 sprigs parsley, chopped	3/4 teaspoon thyme
	Pepper to taste

Arrange sausages on bottom of lightly-greased 8×4-inch loaf pan. Thoroughly mix together remaining ingredients; firmly press into pan. Bake in 350°F oven 1 1/2 hours. Remove from oven; pour off fat. Let stand 10 minutes; invert onto serving plate. Slice to serve.

Baked SPAM and Noodles

4 Servings

An easy oven meal that fills the kitchen with its fragrance.

8 ounces broad egg noodles	1/2 cup milk
1 can (12 ounces) SPAM, diced	1 egg
2 tablespoons butter or margarine, softened	1/8 teaspoon pepper

Break up noodles slightly. Cook according to package directions; drain. Combine hot noodles, SPAM, and butter in greased 1 1/2-quart casserole; stir to melt butter and mix well. Beat together milk, egg, and pepper; pour evenly over top. Bake in 375°F oven 40 minutes.

Linguini Milano
6 Servings

Pasta with a cream sauce — great for a party!

1 pound linguini
1 medium onion, chopped
1 clove garlic, minced
1/4 cup butter or margarine
1 can (12 ounces) SPAM, chopped
2/3 cup heavy cream

1 cup cooked fresh or frozen peas
1/8 teaspoon pepper
3 tablespoons grated Parmesan cheese
Salt

Cook linguini according to package directions; drain. While linguini is cooking, sauté onion and garlic in butter in medium skillet 3 minutes, stirring often. Add SPAM; cook 3 minutes longer. Stir in cream, peas, and pepper; cook, stirring just until sauce simmers. Place cooked linguini in serving bowl; add SPAM mixture and cheese. Toss to mix well; salt to taste. Serve immediately.

Spaghetti Sauce
4 1/2 Cups

Simmer a potful of superb Italian flavor.

1 large onion, chopped
1 large clove garlic, minced
2 tablespoons cooking oil
1 can (35 ounces) Italian tomatoes
1 can (6 ounces) tomato paste
3/4 cup water
1/2 teaspoon basil

1/2 teaspoon oregano
1/2 teaspoon salt
1/2 teaspoon sugar
1/8 teaspoon pepper
1 bay leaf
1 can (12 ounces) SPAM, diced
Parmesan cheese

In large pot, sauté onion and garlic in oil until tender, stirring often. Break up tomatoes or purée in blender; stir into pot with tomato paste, water, and seasonings. Bring to a boil; lower heat and simmer 45 minutes, stirring occasionally. Stir in SPAM; simmer 15 minutes longer. Serve over spaghetti and sprinkle with grated Parmesan cheese, if desired.

Nice to know: This recipe makes enough sauce for a half pound of spaghetti. It can be doubled to serve more than 4, or for hearty appetites.

Cheesy Macaroni Bake

4 Servings

You're never too young or too old to savor this classic.

8 ounces elbow macaroni
1 can (12 ounces) SPAM, diced
2 tablespoons butter or margarine, divided
1 tablespoon flour
1/4 teaspoon salt
1/4 teaspoon dry mustard
Pepper to taste

Dash cayenne
2 cups milk
1/2 pound process sharp American cheese, diced
1/2 cup (1 slice) fresh bread crumbs
1/8 teaspoon paprika

Cook macaroni according to package directions; drain. Combine SPAM with macaroni in lightly-greased 2-quart casserole. In medium saucepan, melt 1 tablespoon butter; blend in flour, salt, mustard, pepper, and cayenne until smooth. Stir in milk; cook over medium heat, stirring until mixture thickens and boils. Add cheese; cook, stirring until cheese melts. Pour over SPAM mixture; mix well. Melt remaining 1 tablespoon butter; combine with bread crumbs and paprika; sprinkle over top. Bake in 400°F oven 20 to 25 minutes.

Microwave directions: Cook macaroni according to package directions. In 4-cup measure, stir together flour, salt, mustard, pepper, and cayenne; slowly mix in milk until smooth. Add 1 tablespoon butter and cheese; microwave 4 minutes. Stir until smooth, microwave 3 minutes more. Beat until smooth. Combine SPAM and macaroni in casserole; mix in sauce. Combine 1 tablespoon butter, bread crumbs, and paprika in 2-cup measure; microwave 1 minute. Reserve. Microwave casserole 3 minutes. Stir; sprinkle with reserved crumb mixture; microwave 2 minutes more. Cover and let stand 3 minutes.

Spaghetti Carbonara   6 Servings

An Italian tradition prepared in minutes.

1 1/2 pounds spaghetti
    1 can (12 ounces) SPAM,
         cubed
   1/2 cup chopped onion
     3 tablespoons olive oil
     3 tablespoons butter or
         margarine

     4 eggs, slightly beaten
   1/2 cup grated Parmesan
         cheese
   1/4 cup chopped parsley
         Salt and pepper to
         taste

Cook spaghetti according to package directions. While spaghetti is cooking, sauté SPAM and onion in oil and butter over medium heat until lightly browned, stirring often; reserve. When spaghetti is cooked, drain quickly and return to pot. Add eggs and toss quickly. Add SPAM mixture, cheese, and parsley; toss lightly to mix well. Season to taste with salt and pepper. Serve immediately.

SPAM Tetrazzini   6 Servings

This dish was originally created for an opera singer named Louisa Tetrazzini — truly a worthy honor!

     8 ounces thin spaghetti
   1/4 cup butter or margarine
   1/4 cup flour
   1/4 teaspoon salt
   1/8 teaspoon pepper
     2 cups water
     2 chicken flavor bouillon
         cubes
     1 cup light cream

     1 can (12 ounces) SPAM,
         diced
     1 can (4 ounces) sliced
         mushrooms, drained
     4 tablespoons grated
         Parmesan cheese,
         divided

Cook spaghetti according to package directions; drain. In medium saucepan, melt butter; blend in flour, salt, and pepper. Stir in water and bouillon cubes; cook and stir over medium heat until mixture thickens and boils. Remove from heat; mix in cream, SPAM, mushrooms, and 2 tablespoons cheese. Combine sauce and spaghetti; turn into lightly-greased 2-quart casserole. Sprinkle remaining cheese over top of casserole. Bake in 425°F oven 30 minutes, or until bubbly and lightly browned top.

Baked Hormel Canned Ham

Easy directions for ham baked to tender juiciness.

Conventional Heating

General Directions: Place ham on rack in baking dish. Bake, uncovered, in preheated 325°F oven until internal temperature reaches 130°F. Baste with sauce or liquid from ham, if desired, during last 30 minutes baking time.

Microwave Oven Heating

General Directions: Place ham on rack or inverted saucer in baking dish. Microwave, uncovered, on roast cycle, until internal temperature reaches 120°F. Cover or tent with aluminum foil and let stand 10 minutes before slicing.

Size	Conventional Time	Microwave Time
1 1/2 pounds (from room temperature)	20 to 25 minutes	7 to 9 minutes
3 pounds (from refrigerator temperature)	1 hour and 15 minutes	15 minutes turn ham over, cook 10 to 12 minutes longer
4 pounds (from refrigerator temperature)	1 hour and 30 minutes	20 minutes turn ham over, cook 18 to 20 minutes longer
5 pounds (from refrigerator temperature)	1 hour and 45 minutes	25 minutes turn ham over, cook 27 to 30 minutes longer

Nice to know: If large hams develop dark spots at edges during microwave cooking, cover spots with small pieces of aluminum foil to prevent further cooking.

Sauces for Baked Ham

If you can't decide which of these luscious fruit sauces to make, you might offer diners a choice of two or three. Serve warm over ham.

Apple Cider Sauce   About 3 cups

1 can (6 ounces) frozen
   apple cider concentrate,
   thawed
3 tablespoons light brown
   sugar
2 tablespoons butter or
   margarine

1/4 teaspoon cinnamon
2 whole cloves
1 1/2 cups water, divided
2 tablespoons cornstarch
2 tablespoons raisins
1/2 teaspoon lemon juice

In small saucepan, combine cider, sugar, butter, cinnamon, and cloves. Stir 1/4 cup water and cornstarch together until smooth; stir into saucepan with remaining water. Cook over medium heat, stirring until mixture thickens and boils. Add raisins and lemon juice; simmer 2 minutes longer.

Microwave directions: In 4-cup glass measure, stir sugar, cinnamon, cloves, and cornstarch until well mixed. Add cider and water; stir. Microwave 5 minutes. Add butter, raisins, and lemon juice; microwave 1/2 minute.

Cherry Jubilee Sauce   About 2 cups

1 can (16 1/2 ounces) pitted
   dark sweet cherries
2 teaspoons cornstarch

1 tablespoon frozen
   orange juice
   concentrate, thawed
2 tablespoons brandy

Drain cherries reserving syrup. Stir about 2 tablespoons syrup with cornstarch until smooth; combine with remaining syrup and orange juice in saucepan. Cook over medium heat, stirring until mixture thickens and boils. Add cherries and brandy; simmer 2 minutes longer.

Microwave directions: Drain cherries reserving syrup. In 4-cup glass measure, mix together cornstarch and orange juice; stir in cherry syrup. Microwave 2 minutes. Add cherries and brandy; microwave 1 minute.

Cranberry Tangerine Sauce   About 2 cups

1 can (16 ounces) whole
     cranberry sauce
1/4 cup frozen tangerine juice
     concentrate, thawed

1 tablespoon sugar
1/8 teaspoon allspice

Combine all ingredients in small saucepan. Bring to boil, stirring occasionally. Lower heat and simmer 2 minutes.

Microwave directions: Combine all ingredients in 4-cup glass measure; stir to mix well. Microwave 3 minutes.

Pineapple Almond Sauce   About 2 1/2 cups

1 can (20 ounces) crushed
     pineapple in syrup
1/3 cup pancake syrup

2 tablespoons slivered
     almonds
Dash ground cloves

Combine all ingredients in small saucepan. Bring to boil, stirring occasionally. Lower heat and simmer 2 minutes.

Microwave directions: Combine all ingredients in 4-cup glass measure; stir to mix well. Microwave 4 minutes.

Raisin Growers' Raisin Sauce   About 2 cups

1 cup raisins
1 3/4 cups water
1/3 cup firmly-packed brown
     sugar
1 1/2 tablespoons cornstarch

1/4 teaspoon cinnamon
1/4 teaspoon ground cloves
1/4 teaspoon dry mustard
1/4 teaspoon salt
1 tablespoon vinegar

In small saucepan, gently boil raisins in water 5 minutes. Mix sugar, cornstarch, cinnamon, cloves, mustard, and salt; stir into raisin mixture. Cook over medium heat, stirring until mixture thickens and boils. Mix in vinegar.

Microwave directions: In 4-cup glass measure, stir sugar, cornstarch, cinnamon, cloves, mustard, and salt until well mixed. Add water and raisins; stir. Microwave 5 minutes. Mix in vinegar.

Summer Skillet Supper

4 Servings

Everything in one skillet — nutrition, flavor, and colorful appeal.

3 medium zucchini (about
　　1 1/2 pounds)
2 tablespoons cooking oil
1 large onion, thinly sliced
1 can (12 ounces) SPAM
1 pound potatoes (3
　　medium), peeled and
　　thinly sliced

1 can (16 ounces)
　　tomatoes
3/4 teaspoon garlic salt
1/2 teaspoon basil
1/2 teaspoon oregano
　　Pepper to taste

Cut zucchini into 1/2-inch slices. Heat oil in large skillet with tight fitting cover. Sauté zucchini and onion over medium-high heat 5 minutes, stirring often. Cut SPAM into 6 slices; halve each slice. Add potatoes and SPAM to skillet; pour tomatoes over all. Sprinkle with garlic salt, basil, oregano, and pepper. Cover and simmer about 25 minutes or until potatoes are tender, stirring after 10 to 20 minutes.

Microwave directions: Combine zucchini, onion, and oil in shallow 10-inch square baking dish; microwave 2 minutes. Stir and microwave 2 minutes more. Cut SPAM into 6 slices; halve each slice. Add SPAM and potatoes; pour tomatoes over all. Sprinkle with seasonings. Cover and microwave 10 minutes until potatoes are tender, turning dish after 4 and 7 minutes. Cover and let stand 5 minutes.

Heidelberg Casserole

6 Servings

Instant hospitality — or a busy-day family dinner.

1 jar (28 ounces) sweet and
   sour red cabbage
2 tablespoons brown sugar,
   divided
1 tablespoon minced onion
   Pinch ground cloves

2 McIntosh apples,
   peeled, cored, and
   diced
1 can (12 ounces) SPAM
1 teaspoon prepared
   mustard

In 1 1/2-quart casserole, stir together red cabbage, 1 tablespoon sugar, onion, and cloves. Mix in apples. Cut SPAM into 6 slices. Stir together remaining sugar and mustard until smooth; spread on SPAM slices. Overlap SPAM on top of cabbage. Bake in 400°F oven 30 minutes, or until cabbage is hot and SPAM glazed.

Microwave directions: Assemble ingredients as above. Microwave 5 minutes. Give casserole 1/4 turn; microwave 3 minutes more. Cover and let stand 3 minutes.

Lentil Cheddar Casserole

6 Servings

What smells so delicious? A lentil casserole on a cold winter day!

1 cup lentils
1 cup chopped onion, divided
1/2 teaspoon thyme
1/4 teaspoon salt
3 cups water
1/2 cup chopped green pepper
2 cloves garlic, minced
2 tablespoons cooking oil

1 can (16 ounces)
   stewed tomatoes
1 can (12 ounces) SPAM,
   diced
1/4 teaspoon pepper
1 cup (4 ounces) shredded
   Cheddar cheese

In small saucepan, combine lentils, 1/2 cup onion, thyme, salt, and water; bring to a boil. Lower heat and stir; cover and simmer about 40 minutes or until lentils are tender and almost all water is absorbed. Sauté green pepper, garlic, and remaining onion in oil until tender; add tomatoes, SPAM, and pepper. In 9-inch square greased baking dish, combine lentils and SPAM mixture. Sprinkle with shredded cheese. Bake in 350°F oven 45 minutes.

Ranchero Casserole

6 Servings

A corn muffin crust tops it off — a casserole youngsters will clamor for!

- 1 cup chopped onion
- 1 cup chopped green pepper
- 1 large clove garlic, minced
- 2 tablespoons cooking oil
- 1 can (16 ounces) tomato sauce
- 1 can (12 ounces) SPAM, diced
- 2 teaspoons chili powder

- 1/4 teaspoon oregano
- Pepper to taste
- 4 ounces American cheese, diced
- 1 can (12 ounces) whole-kernel corn, drained
- 1 package (12 ounces) corn muffin mix
- 2/3 cup milk
- 1 egg

In medium saucepan, sauté onion, green pepper, and garlic in oil until tender but not browned. Stir in tomato sauce, SPAM, chili powder, oregano, and pepper; bring to a boil. Lower heat and simmer, uncovered, 10 minutes. Pour into 11×7×2-inch baking dish. Stir in cheese until melted. Mix in corn. In small bowl, combine muffin mix, milk, and egg until dry ingredients are moistened (mixture will be slightly lumpy). Spoon mixture evenly over surface of casserole. Bake in 400°F oven about 15 minutes, or until lightly browned.

Bavarian Cabbage

4 Servings

Slightly tart, slightly sweet — and completely irresistible!

- 1 large onion, coarsely chopped
- 2 tablespoons butter or margarine
- 1 medium-size head cabbage, coarsely shredded (about 2 pounds)
- 1 can (7 ounces) SPAM, diced

- 1/2 cup water
- 1/2 teaspoon caraway seeds
- 1/2 teaspoon salt
- 1/8 teaspoon pepper
- 2 tablespoons vinegar
- 2 teaspoons sugar

In large saucepan, sauté onion in butter until golden brown, stirring often. Add cabbage, SPAM, water, caraway seeds, salt, and pepper. Bring to a boil; cover and simmer 10 minutes. Stir in vinegar and sugar; mix well.

Baked Zucchini Boats

6 Servings

A great way to serve garden abundance.

6 plump zucchini (about
      2 1/2 pounds)
1 large onion, chopped
2 tablespoons butter or
      margarine
2 tablespoons long-grain
      rice

1/4 teaspoon salt
1/8 teaspoon pepper
1/3 cup grated Cheddar
      cheese
1/4 cup chopped parsley
1 can (12 ounces) SPAM,
      cubed

Halve zucchini lengthwise; scoop out centers leaving a 1/4-inch shell. Chop pulp. In medium skillet, sauté onion and chopped zucchini in butter 3 minutes. Sprinkle rice, salt, and pepper over top; mix well. Cover tightly and simmer 10 minutes, stirring once or twice. Mix in cheese and parsley. Spoon mixture into scooped-out shells. Place in lightly-greased baking dish just large enough to hold squash. Set SPAM into stuffing. Cover pan with foil. Bake in 350°F oven 45 minutes, or until squash is tender.

Puffed Baked Eggplant

4 Servings

A marvelous trick – eggplants "souffléed" and served in their own shells.

2 medium eggplants (3/4
      pound each)
3/4 cup water
4 eggs, separated
1 can (7 ounces) SPAM,
      finely chopped
1/2 cup soft bread crumbs

1/3 cup grated Parmesan
      cheese
1/4 teaspoon garlic salt
1/8 teaspoon nutmeg
1/8 teaspoon pepper

Halve each eggplant lengthwise. Scoop out pulp leaving a 1/4-inch shell. Coarsely chop pulp; cook in water in small covered saucepan 15 minutes or until tender; drain if necessary. Mash cooked pulp; stir in egg yolks. Mix in SPAM, bread crumbs, cheese, garlic salt, nutmeg, and pepper. Whip egg whites until stiff but not dry; fold into SPAM mixture. Pile into eggplant shells; place in baking dish just large enough to hold them. Bake in 325°F oven 35 to 40 minutes, or until puffed and lightly browned.

Creole Beans

6 Servings

From New Orleans — kidney beans hot and tempting!

1 can (12 ounces) SPAM,
  cubed
1 cup chopped onions
1/2 cup chopped green pepper
1 clove garlic, minced
2 tablespoons butter or
  margarine

2 cans (16 ounces each)
  kidney beans, drained
1 can (15 ounces) tomato
  sauce
1 bay leaf, crumbled
Few drops hot
  pepper sauce

In large pot, sauté SPAM, onions, green pepper, and garlic in butter until tender, stirring often. Add remaining ingredients; bring to boil. Transfer to buttered 2-quart casserole. Bake in 350°F oven 40 minutes.

Stuffed Cabbage

6 Servings

Old-fashioned flavors simmered to perfection.

1/2 cup long-grain rice
1 cup chopped onions
2 tablespoons butter or
  margarine
1 can (12 ounces) SPAM,
  chopped
1 can (8 ounces) tomatoes,
  divided

1/8 teaspoon pepper
1 medium-size head cabbage
  (about 2 pounds)
1 can (10 3/4 ounces)
  condensed tomato soup
1 soup can water
1 bay leaf

Cook rice in lightly-salted boiling water 5 minutes; drain. Sauté onions in butter until browned. Combine SPAM, rice, 3/4 of the onions, 1/2 cup tomatoes, and pepper; reserve. In large pot, submerge cabbage in boiling water; peel off leaves as they soften. Pare thin center rib of each cabbage leaf to make rib thinner and easier to roll. Place about 1/4 cup SPAM mixture on each leaf; roll up tucking sides in toward center while rolling to make compact "package." Place stuffed cabbage closely together in pot. Combine remaining tomatoes and onions, tomato soup, water, and bay leaf; pour over cabbage. Bring to a boil, lower heat; cover and simmer 1 hour.

Lazy Day Casserole

8 Servings

Hospitality is always on hand with the ingredients for this creamy casserole.

1 package (10 ounces) frozen
    spinach
8 ounces medium egg
    noodles
2 tablespoons butter or
    margarine
2 tablespoons flour
1 1/3 cups milk

1/2 teaspoon salt
1 cup dairy sour cream
1 can (12 ounces) SPAM,
    cut into strips
1 package (10 ounces)
    frozen peas, thawed
Paprika

Cook spinach according to package directions; drain well. Spread spinach over bottom of lightly greased 13×9-inch baking dish. Cook noodles according to package directions; drain. While noodles are cooking melt butter in medium saucepan; blend in flour until smooth. Add milk, salt, and pepper; cook and stir over medium heat until mixture thickens and boils. Stir a little hot mixture into sour cream; return to pan. Add SPAM and peas. Combine sauce and noodles; pour over spinach. Sprinkle with paprika. Cover and bake in 375°F oven 20 minutes. Uncover and bake 20 minutes longer.

Orange-Yam Bake

4 to 6 Servings

A good recipe to mate with holiday hams and roasts.

1 1/2 pounds yams (about 4
    medium), unpeeled
2 eggs, separated
3 tablespoons orange
    marmalade
Dash ground cloves

1 can (7 ounces) SPAM,
    diced
1 can (11 ounces)
    mandarin orange
    segments, drained
Dash salt

Cook yams in water until tender; drain and peel. Mash yams; mix in egg yolks, marmalade, and cloves. Add SPAM and orange segments; stir gently to mix well. Beat egg whites with salt until stiff but not dry; fold into SPAM mixture. Pile into lightly-greased 1-quart baking dish. Bake in 375°F oven 30 minutes.

Lazy Day Casserole, Barbecued Kabobs (page 76)

Barbecued Kabobs

4 Servings

Complete relaxation — whole-meal kabobs broiled with a quick zesty sauce!

1/4 cup minced onion	4 small red potatoes,
2 tablespoons cooking oil	halved
1 can (6 ounces) tomato	1 large green pepper
juice	2 small onions
1 tablespoon brown sugar	1 can (12 ounces) SPAM,
1 tablespoon cider vinegar	cubed
Dash cayenne	8 mushrooms

In small saucepan, sauté onion in oil until transparent. Add tomato juice, brown sugar, vinegar, and cayenne; bring to a boil. Lower heat and simmer barbecue sauce, uncovered, 10 minutes. Wash potatoes but do not peel. Cook in small amount boiling salted water until tender; drain. Seed and cut green pepper into 16 pieces. Cut each onion into 4 wedges. Alternate potato, green pepper, SPAM, mushrooms, and onions on long skewers. Place on broiling pan; brush with barbecue sauce. Broil at least 3 inches from heat source 15 minutes, turning and brushing with sauce after 5 and 10 minutes.

Best Ever Baked Beans

6 Servings

The right seasonings transform canned baked beans.

2 medium onions, chopped	1 tablespoon chili sauce
1 tablespoon butter or	1 tablespoon molasses
margarine	1/2 teaspoon chili powder
2 cans (1 pound each)	1 can (12 ounces) SPAM,
vegetarian beans in	cubed
tomato sauce	

Sauté onions in butter until transparent. In 1 1/2-quart casserole, combine onions, beans, chili sauce, molasses, and chili powder; stir to mix well. Stir in SPAM. Cover and bake in 400°F oven 35 minutes.

Microwave directions: Combine onions and butter in 1 1/2-quart casserole; microwave 2 minutes. Stir; microwave 2 minutes more. Add remaining ingredients. Microwave 10 minutes, stirring after 4 and 8 minutes. Cover and let stand 5 minutes.

Cauliflower au Gratin

4 Servings

Pale cauliflower brightened with a golden sauce.

1 head (about 1 1/2 pounds) cauliflower	1/8 teaspoon pepper
3 tablespoons butter or margarine	1 3/4 cups milk
3 tablespoons flour	1 can (12 ounces) SPAM, cubed
1/8 teaspoon salt	1/2 cup shredded Swiss cheese

Separate cauliflower into small flowerettes. Cook in small amount boiling salted water until tender; drain. In medium saucepan, melt butter; blend in flour, salt, and pepper until smooth. Mix in milk. Cook over medium heat, stirring until mixture thickens and boils. Mix in SPAM. Place cauliflower in lightly-greased 1 1/2-quart baking dish. Pour on SPAM mixture; stir to mix well. Sprinkle cheese over top. Bake in 450°F oven 8 to 10 minutes, until lightly browned on top.

Microwave directions: Place cauliflowerettes, 1/4 cup water, and 1/4 teaspoon butter in 1 1/2-quart casserole; cover and microwave 8 minutes, stirring after 4 minutes. In 4-cup measure, stir together flour, salt, and pepper; slowly mix in milk until smooth. Microwave 3 minutes. Mix until smooth; microwave 2 minutes more. Stir until smooth. Add SPAM to casserole; pour sauce over. Microwave 3 minutes. Stir; sprinkle with cheese and microwave 2 minutes more. Cover and let stand 2 minutes.

Savory Potato Bake

4 Servings

Mashed potatoes taken a delicious step further.

1 pound potatoes (3 medium)	2 tablespoons grated Parmesan cheese, divided
1 can (7 ounces) SPAM, diced	
1/2 cup chopped fresh parsley	Pepper to taste
1 clove garlic, minced	1 egg yolk

Cook potatoes in small amount boiling salted water until tender; drain. Mash potatoes well; mix in SPAM, parsley, garlic, 1 tablespoon cheese, pepper, and egg yolk. Spread mixture in lightly-greased 1-quart baking dish. Sprinkle with remaining cheese. Bake in 425°F oven 15 minutes. Place under broiler to brown, if desired.

Baked Stuffed Tomatoes   6 Servings

Easy glamour for harvest bounty.

6 large tomatoes (about
    2 1/2 pounds)
2 small zucchini, diced
    (about 3/4 pound)
1 large onion, chopped
1 large clove garlic,
    minced

3 tablespoons butter or
    margarine
1 can (7 ounces) SPAM,
    diced
1/2 teaspoon basil
1/8 teaspoon pepper
1/2 cup croutons

Cut a thin slice from top of tomatoes; scoop out centers leaving a 1/4-inch shell. Finely chop tomato pulp; reserve. In large skillet, sauté zucchini, onion, and garlic in butter 3 minutes, stirring often. Add SPAM, tomato pulp, basil, and pepper; stir to mix. Bring to boil; lower heat and simmer uncovered until liquid evaporates, stirring occasionally. Cool to room temperature. Mix in croutons. Spoon filling into tomato shells. Place tomatoes in baking dish; bake in 375°F oven 20 minutes. Serve hot or at room temperature.

Confetti Hash Peppers   3 Servings

For a family celebration — or a good reason to celebrate!

3 medium green peppers
    (about 3/4 pound)
1 can (15 ounces) Mary
    Kitchen Roast Beef Hash
1/2 cup frozen whole-kernel
    corn, thawed

1/4 cup chopped onion
2 tablespoons chili
    sauce
1/3 cup shredded Cheddar
    cheese

Cut off tops of peppers; remove seeds. Cook in boiling water to cover 3 minutes; drain. Combine hash, corn, onion, and chili sauce; pile into pepper halves. Place peppers in lightly-greased baking dish. Bake in 375°F oven 20 minutes. Sprinkle with cheese; bake 10 minutes longer.

Microwave directions: Cut off tops of peppers; remove seeds. Place, cut side down, in baking dish. Cover with waxed paper; microwave 2 minutes. Turn dish 1/4 turn; microwave 2 minutes more. Combine hash, corn, onion, and chili sauce; pile into pepper halves. Microwave 2 minutes; turn dish 1/4 turn; microwave 2 minutes more. Sprinkle with cheese; microwave 1 minute. Cover and let stand 5 minutes.

Creamy Succotash Bake

4 Servings

An all-American combination that never loses its appeal.

1 package (10 ounces) frozen
    lima beans
1 can (17 ounces) cream-style
    corn
1/4 cup light cream

1/2 teaspoon dehydrated
    onion flakes
1 can (12 ounces) SPAM
1/3 cup shredded Cheddar
    cheese

Cook lima beans according to package directions until barely tender; drain well. In lightly-greased 8-inch square baking dish, combine lima beans, corn, cream, and onion flakes. Cut SPAM into 8 slices; overlap on top of vegetable mixture. Sprinkle with cheese. Bake in 375°F oven about 30 minutes, or until bubbly hot.

Microwave directions: Place frozen lima beans and 1/4 teaspoon salt in 1 1/2-quart casserole; cover and microwave 7 minutes, stirring after 4 minutes. Mix in corn, cream, and onion flakes. Place SPAM slices on top. Microwave 3 minutes. Sprinkle cheese over top; microwave 1 minute more. Cover and let stand 3 minutes.

Sweet and Sour Green Beans

4 Servings

A simple shortcut to a deluxe side dish.

2 packages (9 ounces each)
    frozen cut green beans
1/4 cup chopped onion
2 tablespoons butter or
    margarine
1 tablespoon flour

1/2 cup dairy sour cream
1 can (7 ounces) SPAM,
    cut in strips
1 teaspoon vinegar
Dash pepper

In medium saucepan, cook beans in salted water according to package directons until tender crisp. Remove beans. Drain cooking liquid, reserving 2/3 cup. In same saucepan, sauté onion in butter until transparent, stirring often. Blend in flour until smooth; stir in reserved cooking liquid. Cook over medium heat, stirring until mixture thickens and boils. Mix in sour cream until smooth. Add SPAM, beans, vinegar, and pepper. Cook and stir until heated.

Stuffed Acorn Squash

4 Servings

The tantalizing sweetness of acorn squash dressed up in Sunday-dinner best.

2 acorn squash (about 1 pound)
1 small onion, finely chopped
2 tablespoons butter or margarine
1 tablespoon flour

1/8 teaspoon salt
1/8 teaspoon pepper
1/3 cup milk
1 can (7 ounces) SPAM, diced
1 cup fresh or frozen peas, cooked

Halve squash lengthwise; scrape out seeds. Place squash, cut side down, in lightly-greased baking dish. Bake in 350°F oven 45 minutes. While squash is baking, in small saucepan, sauté onion in butter until transparent. Blend in flour, salt, and pepper until smooth. Mix in milk; cook over medium heat, stirring until mixture thickens and boils. Remove from heat; stir in SPAM and peas. Spoon mixture into squash halves. Cover and return to oven for 5 to 10 minutes until SPAM is piping hot.

Microwave directions: Pierce squash; microwave 10 minutes until tender. Halve and remove seeds. In 2-cup measure, combine butter with onion; microwave 1 minute. Blend in flour; mix in milk, salt, and pepper until smooth. Microwave 1 minute; mix well until smooth. Combine SPAM, peas, and sauce; pile into squash halves. Microwave 3 minutes. Cover and let stand 3 minutes.

Potatoes au Gratin

4 Servings

An attractive casserole that cooks itself!

1 package (5 1/2 ounces) potatoes au gratin mix
1 can (7 ounces) SPAM, diced

1/4 cup chopped green pepper
2 cups boiling water
2/3 cup milk
1 medium tomato

In 1 1/2-quart casserole, combine potatoes, sauce mix, SPAM, and green pepper. Pour in boiling water and milk; stir to mix well. Bake, uncovered, in 400°F oven 25 minutes. Stir well. Slice tomato; halve each slice. Overlap tomato slices on top of casserole. Return to oven and bake 10 minutes longer. Let stand 5 minutes before serving.

Yam Croquettes with Pineapple Sauce

3 Servings

A real treat — crunchy croquettes with a smooth fruity sauce!

1 can (16 ounces) cut yams
1 can (7 ounces) SPAM,
   finely chopped
1 egg yolk
   Pepper to taste

1/2 cup bread crumbs
1 egg, slightly beaten
   Shortening
   Pineapple Sauce
   (below)

Drain yams and mash. Combine with SPAM, egg yolk, and pepper. Shape mixture into 6 balls. Roll in bread crumbs; dip in beaten egg. Roll in bread crumbs again. Refrigerate at least 1 hour for easy frying. Heat 3 inches shortening to 350°F; slip in croquettes. Cook 3 to 4 minutes, until browned. Drain on paper towels. Serve with Pineapple Sauce.

Pineapple Sauce

1/4 cup water
1 teaspoon cornstarch
1 can (8 ounces) crushed
   pineapple in syrup

2 tablespoons dark
   brown sugar
2 whole cloves

In small saucepan, stir together water and cornstarch until smooth. Add pineapple, sugar, and cloves. Cook and stir over medium heat until mixture thickens and boils. Simmer 2 minutes; remove cloves before serving.

Baked Beans Latino   4 Servings

Deeply flavored pinto beans enriched with mellow Monterey Jack cheese.

8 ounces dried pinto beans
1 can (8 ounces) tomato
    sauce
2 tablespoons cooking oil
1 medium onion, coarsely
    chopped
1 clove garlic, minced
1 teaspoon salt
1/2 teaspoon cumin
1 can (7 ounces) SPAM,
    diced
1/3 cup shredded Monterey
    Jack cheese

Wash and pick over beans. In medium saucepan combine beans, tomato sauce, oil, onion, garlic, salt, and cumin. Completely cover beans with water. Heat to boiling; cover and simmer, stirring occasionally, about 1 1/4 to 1 1/2 hours or until beans are tender. Add water if necessary to keep beans covered while cooking. Transfer mixture to 1 1/2-quart casserole; mix in SPAM. Bake in 350°F oven 40 minutes. Sprinkle with cheese; return to oven 5 minutes longer.

Reuben Baked Potatoes   4 Servings

Wow! Baked potatoes topped with everything good!

4 large baking potatoes
    (about 2 pounds)
    Cooking oil
1 can (7 ounces) SPAM,
    diced
1/2 cup sauerkraut,
    rinsed and drained
1/2 cup shredded Swiss
    cheese

Wash potatoes well; rub with cooking oil. Bake in 425°F oven 45 minutes or until tender. Remove from oven; cut a cross in top and push ends together to open. Toss SPAM with sauerkraut. Mound SPAM mixture on top of potatoes; sprinkle with cheese. Return to oven for 5 to 7 minutes until SPAM is hot and cheese melts.

Microwave directions: Scrub potatoes; prick with fork. Microwave 10 to 12 minutes until tender. Cut a cross in top and push ends together to open. Toss together SPAM, sauerkraut, and cheese; mound mixture on top of potatoes. Microwave 5 minutes.

Potato Scallop

4 to 6 Servings

A whole meal baked in a creamy hot casserole.

2 pounds potatoes
  (6 medium)
4 tablespoons butter or
  margarine, divided
3 tablespoons flour
2 teaspoons prepared
  mustard
1/2 teaspoon salt

1/8 teaspoon pepper
1 3/4 cups milk
1/4 cup chopped green
  onions
1 can (12 ounces) SPAM
1 cup frozen peas,
  cooked

Cook potatoes in boiling salted water until tender; drain. Cool to room temperature; peel and slice. In medium saucepan, melt 3 tablespoons butter; blend in flour, mustard, salt, and pepper; stir in milk. Cook over medium heat, stirring until mixture thickens and boils; add onions. In lightly-greased 2-quart casserole, layer mustard sauce and potatoes, beginning and ending with sauce. Cover and bake in 375°F oven 20 minutes. Cut SPAM into 6 slices; halve each slice. Remove casserole from oven; overlap SPAM around edge of casserole; pile peas in center. Dot with remaining tablespoon butter. Cover and bake 15 minutes longer, or until bubbly hot.

Nice to know: The potatoes can be boiled the day before.

Rice Stuffing

For a 3 1/2- to 4-pound chicken

A wonderful herb-seasoned stuffing for a plump, juicy roast chicken.

1/2 cup long-grain rice
1/3 cup chopped onion
1/4 cup chopped celery
1 tablespoon butter or
  margarine
1 can (7 ounces) SPAM,
  finely chopped

1/4 cup marinara sauce,
  canned or homemade
  (page 100)
1/2 teaspoon rosemary
Pepper to taste

Cook rice according to package directions; reserve. In medium skillet, sauté onion and celery in butter until tender. Stir SPAM into skillet with marinara sauce, rosemary, and pepper. Mix in rice. Spoon into body cavity of chicken; truss and roast as usual.

Cantonese Sweet and Sour   4 Servings

Family and guests alike will look forward to this Chinese favorite.

1 large carrot, sliced
  diagonally
2 green onions
2 tablespoons cooking oil
1 clove garlic, minced
1 small cucumber, cut in
  chunks
2/3 cup water, divided
1 tablespoon cornstarch

3 tablespoons sugar
3 tablespoons catsup
3 tablespoons vinegar
1 teaspoon soy sauce
1 can (12 ounces) SPAM,
  cut in chunks
1 can (8 ounces) bamboo
  shoots, drained

Cook carrot in small amount salted boiling water just until tender crisp; drain. Rinse with cold water; reserve. Cut onions into 2-inch lengths; then into thin long pieces. In wok or large skillet, heat oil; add garlic and sauté until lightly browned. Add cucumber and onions; cook and stir over high heat 2 minutes. Stir a little water into cornstarch to make a smooth paste; stir in remaining water, sugar, vinegar, catsup, and soy sauce. Add to wok; cook and stir until mixture thickens and boils. Add SPAM, bamboo shoots, and reserved carrots; cook and stir to serving temperature. Serve over hot rice.

Fried Rice   2 to 3 Servings

Whether you serve Fried Rice as a main course or a side dish, everyone will want seconds!

1/4 cup cooking oil
1 can (6 3/4 ounces) Hormel
  Chunk Ham, drained
4 cups cold cooked rice

1/4 cup thinly-sliced
  green onions
2 eggs, beaten
1 tablespoon soy sauce

In wok or large skillet, heat oil until hot; add ham and cook 2 minutes, stirring often. With slotted spoon, remove ham and reserve. Add rice and onions to wok; cook over medium heat about 4 minutes, stirring constantly to separate grains. (Do not brown rice.) Pour eggs over rice; cook and stir until eggs are set. Add ham and soy sauce; cook and stir just until heated and well mixed.

Bacon 'n Cheese
Baked Potatoes

4 Servings

A saucy topping sure to tease appetites.

4 baking potatoes (about 2
  pounds)
Cooking oil
2 tablespoons butter or
  margarine
2 tablespoons flour
1/2 teaspoon salt
1/4 teaspoon Worcestershire
  sauce

1/8 teaspoon dry mustard
1/8 teaspoon pepper
1 1/2 cups milk
3/4 cup shredded Cheddar
  cheese
1/4 cup Hormel Bacon Bits

Wash potatoes well; rub with cooking oil. Bake in 425°F oven about 45 minutes, or until tender. While potatoes are baking, melt butter in medium saucepan; blend in flour, salt, Worcestershire, mustard, and pepper until smooth. Add milk; cook and stir over medium heat until mixture thickens and boils. Stir in cheese; cook and stir until cheese melts. Just before serving, stir in bacon. Cut a cross into top of potatoes and push ends together to open; serve with bacon-cheese sauce. Sprinkle additional bacon to garnish.

Microwave directions: Scrub potatoes; prick and place in microwave oven. Microwave 12 minutes, or until tender. Remove from oven. In 4-cup measure, mix flour, salt, Worcestershire, mustard, and pepper. Gradually mix in milk; beat until smooth. Mix in cheese and butter. Microwave 3 minutes. Beat well; microwave 3 minutes longer, or until thickened. Beat until smooth; stir in bacon. Prepare potatoes with sauce as above.

Come On Over!

There are so many ways to spend time with friends. You can casually invite them for Chicken Cacciatore, a big pan of Lasagna, or glazed Double Pork Loaf. You can celebrate a birthday or anniversary with Stuffed Flank Steak Verona. You can plan a glittering buffet of Gala Frosted Ham, Baked Deviled Mushrooms, Far East Appetizer Meatballs, and Hawaiian Kabobs. Or you can set aside an evening for relaxed conversation, with Guacamole Dip and Pizza Olé. Youngsters, teen-agers, busy folks, and family, too — everyone enjoys a party! And there are recipes to match every party mood in this entertaining chapter.

Cheese Ball
One 1 1/2 pound ball

Remember this brightly-colored cheese ball when it's time for holiday entertaining.

1 can (7 ounces) SPAM
2 cups shredded Cheddar cheese
1 package (3 ounces) cream cheese, softened
1/2 teaspoon dehydrated onion flakes, crumbled
1/2 teaspoon Worcestershire sauce
1/8 teaspoon dry mustard
1/8 teaspoon chili powder
Chopped parsley
Paprika

Finely chop SPAM or process in food processor using chopping blade. In medium bowl, combine SPAM and remaining ingredients until well mixed. Cover and refrigerate about 1 hour to firm. Shape into a ball; wrap in waxed paper and refrigerate until serving time. Roll ball in chopped parsley or paprika. Place on serving tray and circle with crackers.

Curried-Turkey Stuffed Mushrooms
2 Servings

A guest of honor for impressive luncheons.

8 large mushrooms
1 tablespoon finely-chopped onion
1 tablespoon finely-chopped celery
2 tablespoons butter or margarine, divided

1 can (6 3/4 ounces) Hormel Chunk Turkey, flaked
1 teaspoon curry powder
1/2 teaspoon lemon juice
1/8 teaspoon garlic salt

Wash mushrooms; remove stems. Sauté onion and celery in 1 tablespoon butter until onion is transparent. Mix in turkey, curry powder, lemon juice, and garlic salt. Pile turkey mixture into mushroom caps. Place in baking pan; dot with remaining butter. Bake in 375°F oven 15 minutes.

Nice to know: Mushroom stems can be chopped and added to the turkey mixture or you can save them for another use.

Sausage Wrap-Ups
3 to 4 Servings

Two imaginative variations on everyone's favorite piggies-in-blankets.

1 package (8 ounces) refrigerated crescent rolls
1 can (5 ounces) Hormel Vienna Sausages
1 ounce Cheddar cheese, split into 7 strips

1 tablespoon mayonnaise
1 can (5 ounces) Hormel Chicken Vienna Sausages
7 strips green pepper
3 green onions, split into 7 strips

Remove rolls from package; cut each roll into 2 triangles. Make a deep lengthwise cut into Vienna Sausages; fill with cheese strips. Place one cheese-filled sausage on each of 7 triangles; roll up, pinching to seal. Place on ungreased baking sheet. Place a dab of mayonnaise at bottom side of another 7 triangles. Top with Chicken Vienna Sausages; add a strip of green pepper and onion to each. Roll up, pinching to seal. Place on ungreased baking sheet. Bake in 375°F oven about 10 minutes, or until golden brown.

Nice to know: You will have 2 small triangles left. Sprinkle them lightly with Cheddar cheese; roll up and bake with others.

Far East Appetizer Meatballs   8 Servings

The crunch of bean sprouts, a hint of ginger, and the allure of a truly different cocktail meatball.

1 can (12 ounces) SPAM
2/3 cup dry bread crumbs
1/2 cup chopped well-drained
      bean sprouts
1/4 cup chopped green onions
1/4 teaspoon powdered
      ginger

Pepper to taste
Cocktail picks
Far East Dipping
   Sauce (below)

Grind SPAM or process in food processor using chopping blade, until finely chopped. Combine SPAM with bread crumbs, bean sprouts, onion, ginger, and pepper. Using about 1 tablespoon for each meatball, shape mixture into 24 balls. Place on rack in shallow baking pan; bake in 425°F oven 15 minutes. Cool to room temperature. Spear meatballs on cocktail picks and dip into hot Far East Dipping Sauce.

Far East Dipping Sauce

1 cup tomato juice
1/3 cup finely-chopped green
      onions

1/4 cup finely-chopped
      green pepper
1/4 teaspoon ground ginger

In small saucepan, combine all ingredients. Bring to a boil; simmer, uncovered, 5 minutes. Serve hot.

Bacon Stuffed Eggs   12 Appetizers

Crisp bacon in satiny stuffed eggs — a new look for a delicious duo!

6 hard-cooked eggs
1/4 cup mayonnaise
2 tablespoons Hormel
      Bacon Bits

2 tablespoons finely-
      chopped parsley
Dash pepper

Halve eggs lengthwise; scoop out yolks. Thoroughly mash yolks; mix in mayonnaise, bacon, parsley, and pepper. Pile mixture into egg whites; place on serving plate. Cover and refrigerate until chilled. Garnish with a carrot or radish slice, if desired.

Deviled Eggs

12 Servings

Devilishly good before dinner or on a buffet table.

6 eggs, hard-cooked
1 can (3 ounces) Deviled
    SPAM
1 tablespoon plain yogurt

1 tablespoon sweet
    pickle relish
1 teaspoon prepared
    mustard

Shell and halve eggs lengthwise. Remove yolks; mash well. Mix in SPAM, yogurt, relish, and mustard. Gently pile mixture into egg whites. Refrigerate until serving time; sprinkle with paprika, if desired.

Chili Cheese Dip

3 Cups

The life of a party — an exciting chili dip.

4 ounces Cheddar cheese
1 can (15 ounces) Hormel
    Chili - No Beans
8 ounces creamed cottage
    cheese
2 to 3 canned green
    chilies

1/4 teaspoon turmeric
    (optional)
    Black olives
    Tomatoes

Shred Cheddar cheese or process in food processor. Add remaining ingredients; blend until smooth. Cover and refrigerate at least 2 hours to blend flavors. To serve, transfer to serving bowl and garnish top with black olives and chopped tomatoes. Serve with corn chips and crackers.

Turkey Tetrazzini Spread

2 1/3 Cups

The taste of a favorite entrée in an intriguing spread.

1 can (6 3/4 ounces) Hormel
    Chunk Turkey, drained
    and flaked
1 package (8 ounces) cream
    cheese, softened
1 tablespoon sherry

1 teaspoon prepared
    horseradish
1/2 teaspoon Worcester-
    shire sauce
1 cup chopped fresh
    mushrooms (about
    1/4 pound)

Thoroughly blend turkey, cream cheese, sherry, horseradish, and Worcestershire. Gently stir in mushrooms. Spoon into serving bowl. Cover and refrigerate until serving time.

Baked Deviled Mushrooms   4 Servings

Offer an hors d'oeuvre that nobody can resist!

8 large mushrooms (1/2 pound)	1 can (3 ounces) Deviled SPAM
1 tablespoon finely-chopped onion	1 tablespoon bread crumbs
1 tablespoon butter or margarine	

Wash mushrooms; remove stems and finely chop. Sauté chopped stems and onion in butter until tender but not browned. Stir in SPAM and bread crumbs. Pile mixture into mushroom caps; place on baking pan. Bake in 375°F oven 15 minutes.

Microwave directions: In 2-cup baking dish, combine mushrooms stems, onion, and butter. Microwave 3 minutes. Mix in SPAM and bread crumbs. Pile mixture into mushroom caps; place in 9-inch pie plate. Microwave 1 minute. Turn dish 1/4 turn; microwave 1 minute more.

Nice to know: This recipe can be doubled to serve 4 as a main course. When doubling for microwave directions cook two batches separately.

Hawaiian Kabobs   24 Appetizers

Aloha . . . a beautiful greeting, a tempting hors d'oeuvre.

1 can (3 ounces) Deviled SPAM	1/4 teaspoon Worcestershire sauce
4 ounces cream cheese, softened	Chopped parsley
1/4 cup chopped toasted almonds	1 can (8 ounces) pineapple chunks, drained
1/4 teaspoon crushed dehydrated onion flakes	Cocktail picks

Thoroughly mix SPAM, cheese, almonds, onion flakes, and Worcestershire. Cover and refrigerate until firm. Shape mixture into 24 marble-size balls; roll in parsley. If necessary, halve some pineapple chunks to make 24 chunks. Spear a SPAM ball and a pineapple chunk on each cocktail pick.

Party Canapé Pies

40 Canapés

A trio of delicious spreads easily transformed into colorful canapés.

1 small round loaf (about 1
  pound) unsliced
  pumpernickel bread
2 tablespoons butter or
  margarine
Ham-Pickle Spread (below)

Olive-Egg Spread
  (below)
Chicken Spread
  (below)
1 cucumber, peeled and
  chopped

Slice bread crosswise (you should have 5 large circles plus a few smaller ones). Lightly butter large circles. Top bread rounds with alternating circles of Ham-Pickle Spread, Olive-Egg Spread, Chicken Spread, and cucumber. Cut each round into 8 wedges to serve.

Ham-Pickle Spread: Mix 1 can (6 3/4 ounces) Hormel Chunk Ham, drained, 1/2 cup shredded Cheddar cheese, 2 tablespoons sweet pickle relish, and 2 tablespoons mayonnaise.

Olive-Egg Spread: Mix 3 chopped hard-cooked eggs, 2 tablespoons chopped black olives, 2 tablespoons mayonnaise, and 1 teaspoon prepared mustard. Season to taste with salt and pepper.

Chicken Spread: Mix 1 can (6 3/4 ounces) Hormel Chunk Chicken, 1/4 cup finely-chopped celery, 3 tablespoons mayonnaise, and 1 tablespoon chopped raisins.

Gourmet Chicken Spread

1 1/3 Cups

The subtle difference of bleu cheese and slivered Brazil nuts.

1 can (6 3/4 ounces) Hormel
  Chunk Chicken, drained
1 package (3 ounces) cream
  cheese, softened

1 ounce bleu cheese
  Sliced Brazil nuts

Thoroughly blend chicken, cream cheese, and bleu cheese. Spoon into serving bowl. Cover and refrigerate until serving time. Sprinkle with Brazil nuts.

Guacamole Dip

About 2 1/2 cups

A dip that does a quick "disappearing act" at parties!

1 medium fully-ripe avocado
1 tablespoon lemon juice
1 tablespoon chopped onion
1 small clove garlic,
    minced
1/4 teaspoon salt
    Dash pepper

Hot pepper sauce to
    taste
1 can (7 ounces) SPAM,
    finely diced
1 small tomato, peeled
    and chopped

Peel avocado; discard pit. Mash with a fork or process in food processor until smooth. Stir in lemon juice, onion, garlic, salt, pepper, and pepper sauce. Gently stir in SPAM and tomato. Cover and refrigerate until serving time. Serve with crackers or tortilla chips.

Pickled Mushrooms

1 Quart

A little nibble that tempts and tempts and tempts!

3/4 cup vinegar
3/4 cup water
1/4 teaspoon salt
3 peppercorns
2 whole allspice
1 bay leaf

1 whole clove
1 can (12 ounces) SPAM
1 can (8 ounces)
    mushrooms, drained
1 small onion, thinly
    sliced

In small saucepan, combine vinegar, water, salt, peppercorns, allspice, bay leaf, and clove; bring to a boil. Remove from heat; let cool to room temperature. Meanwhile, cut SPAM into strips about 2 inches long and 1/4-inch wide. Alternately layer SPAM, mushrooms, and onion slices in 1-quart jar with a wide mouth. Pour pickling mixture with spices oven SPAM and vegetables. Cover tightly and refrigerate at least 24 hours, shaking or turning jar over occasionally.

Nice to know: A jar of this is great to have on hand for impromptu entertaining; it will keep one week in the refrigerator.

Cheese Canapé Spread

1 1/2 cups

A generous blend of meat and two cheeses.

2 cans (3 ounces each)
    Deviled SPAM
1 package (3 ounces) cream
    cheese, softened

1/2 cup (2 ounces)
    grated Swiss cheese
1 teaspoon prepared
    mustard

Thoroughly blend SPAM, cream cheese, Swiss cheese, and mustard. Spoon into serving bowl. Cover and refrigerate until serving time.

Chicken Cashew
Canapé Spread

1 1/2 Cups

Nothing could be easier — or more appropriate for elegant entertaining.

1 can (6 3/4 ounces) Hormel
    Chunk Chicken, drained
1/2 cup finely-chopped
    cashews
1/4 cup finely-chopped pitted
    black olives

1/3 cup dairy sour cream
Few drops hot
    pepper sauce

Break up chicken with fork. Add cashews, olives, sour cream, and pepper sauce; mix well. Serve with crackers or toast.

Hot Chili Cheese Spread

2 1/2 Cups

Rich flavor belies the simplicity of this spread.

1 can (15 ounces) Hormel
    Chili with Beans

1 cup grated sharp
    process cheese

Combine chili and cheese in small saucepan. Heat until hot and cheese is melted. Serve hot on sesame crackers or party rye.

Chicken Cacciatore   8 Servings

An Italian festival of chicken, herbs, and vegetables.

1 chicken (about 2 1/2 pounds),
   cut into serving pieces
2 tablespoons olive oil
1 cup coarsely-chopped onion
   (1 medium)
1/4 pound mushrooms, sliced
1 large clove garlic,
   minced
1 can (16 ounces) Italian
   tomatoes in tomato
   purée
1/2 cup chicken broth

1/2 cup dry white wine
1/2 teaspoon oregano
1/2 teaspoon rosemary
1/2 teaspoon salt
   Pepper to taste
1 can (12 ounces) SPAM,
   cut into 8 slices
1 package (9 ounces)
   frozen Italian green
   beans, slightly
   thawed

In large skillet over medium heat, brown chicken well in oil. Remove chicken from skillet; pour off all but 2 tablespoons drippings. Add onion, mushrooms, and garlic; sauté until onions are transparent. Mix in tomatoes, broth, wine, oregano, rosemary, salt, and pepper. Add chicken, SPAM, and beans to skillet; spoon sauce over. Bring to a boil; cover and simmer 20 minutes, or until chicken is tender.

Stuffed Turkey Breast   8 Servings

A great stuffing sets the mood of a holiday table.

1/2 cup thinly-sliced celery
1/4 cup chopped onion
1/4 cup butter or margarine
1 can (7 ounces) SPAM,
   diced
1 package (7 ounces)
   stuffing mix

1 cup water
   Salt
1 turkey breast (5 to
   6 pounds)
3 tablespoons melted
   butter or margarine

In medium skillet, sauté celery and onion in butter until onion is transparent; mix in SPAM. Stir mixture into stuffing mix. Gradually add water, mixing constantly. Lightly salt inside cavity of turkey breast; spoon stuffing into cavity. Cover open surface of stuffing with piece of aluminum foil. Place turkey breast, skin side up, on rack in shallow baking pan; sprinkle lightly with salt and brush with melted butter. Roast in 350°F oven about 2 1/2 hours, or until tender, basting occasionally.

Mexicale Casserole

4 to 6 Servings

Wonderful for a casual get-together of youngsters and the young-at-heart!

1/2 cup chopped celery
1/4 cup chopped green pepper
2 tablespoons butter or margarine
1 can (15 ounces) Hormel Tamales

1 can (15 ounces) Hormel Chili - No Beans
1/2 cup shredded Cheddar cheese
1 package (8 1/2 ounces) corn muffin mix

In small skillet, sauté celery and green pepper in butter until tender. Remove papers from tamales and slice into bite-size pieces. Combine tamales, chili, celery, and green pepper. Pour half of mixture into 8- or 9-inch baking dish. Sprinkle with cheese and top with remaining mixture. Prepare corn muffin mix according to package directions; drop batter by spoonfuls over top of mixture. Bake in 375°F oven 25 minutes.

Choucroute

8 to 10 Servings

A one-pot crowd pleaser full of hearty, Old World flavor.

1/2 pound Italian sausages
1 can (5 ounces) Hormel Chicken Vienna sausages
2 cups chopped onions
1 large clove garlic, minced
3 pounds sauerkraut, rinsed and drained
1 1/2 cups beer

1 cup water
1 apple, peeled, cored, and chopped
4 peppercorns
3 cloves
1 bay leaf
1 can (12 ounces) SPAM
1/2 pound kielbasa

In large skillet (at least 10 inches in diameter), brown sausages on all sides over low heat. Remove from skillet; drain off all but 2 tablespoons drippings. Sauté onions and garlic over medium heat until onions are lightly browned, stirring often. Add sauerkraut, beer, water, and apple; bring to a boil. Tie peppercorns, cloves, and bay leaf together in a piece of cheesecloth; add to skillet. Cut SPAM into 6 slices; stir into sauerkraut mixture with kielbasa, and sausages. Lower heat; cover and simmer 2 hours. Discard cheesecloth bag before serving.

Nice to know: Hormel Italian Sausage is the perfect partner to Choucroute. Available in your meat department.

Gala Frosted Ham

6 Servings

Fresh appeal — vegetable "flowers" delicately strewn on a "field" of cream cheese frosting.

1 package (8 ounces) cream cheese, softened	1 1/2 pound Hormel Canned Ham
2 tablespoons prepared horseradish	Carrot slices
	Pitted black olives
2 tablespoons plain yogurt	Fresh chives or thin
1/8 teaspoon celery salt	green pepper strips

Thoroughly blend cream cheese, horseradish, yogurt and celery salt until well mixed. Place ham on serving plate; frost with cream cheese mixture. Arrange carrot stars with olive centers; finish with "stems" of chives or green pepper. Cover and refrigerate until serving time.

Nice to know: Hormel Canned Ham in the 1 1/2 pound size is stored in the cupboard or pantry. It never needs refrigeration! Keep several on hand for "surprise" guests or last-minute meals.

Gala Frosted Ham

Baked Eggplant Italiano

4 Servings

Greet guests with the fabulous aromas of bubbly hot eggplant, sauce, and cheese.

1 eggplant (about 1 1/4 pounds)	1 1/2 cups (6 ounces), shredded mozzarella cheese, divided
Salt	
Flour	1 can (7 ounces) SPAM, diced
2 eggs, well beaten	
Cooking oil	1 cup Marinara Sauce (below)

Cut unpeeled eggplant lengthwise in 1/4-inch slices. Lightly salt and place on plate; place a baking pan filled with heavy cans on top of eggplant. Let stand 1 hour; drain off accumulated liquid. Dip each slice in flour, then into beaten eggs. Sauté in oil in large skillet, a few slices at a time, until browned on both sides. Drain on paper towel. Reserve about 1/3 cup mozzarella cheese; combine remaining cheese with SPAM. Spread about 2 tablespoons sauce over bottom of lightly-greased 1-quart baking dish. Cover with a layer of eggplant. Add layer of SPAM mixture; spread with sauce. Repeat layers ending with sauce. Sprinkle with reserved cheese. Bake in 400°F oven 15 minutes, or until mixture is hot and cheese melts on top. Let stand 5 minutes before cutting.

Marinara Sauce

1/4 cup chopped onion	2 tablespoons red wine
1/4 cup chopped celery	1/4 teaspoon basil
1 clove garlic, minced	1/4 teaspoon oregano
1 tablespoon pure vegetable oil	1/4 teaspoon salt
	1/8 teaspoon pepper
1 can (15 ounces) tomato sauce	1 bay leaf

In a medium saucepan, sauté onion, celery, and garlic in oil. Add remaining ingredients and simmer 15 minutes.

Nice to know: You'll have an extra cup of sauce. Freeze it and use another day for Rice Stuffing (page 83).

Jambalaya

6 Servings

A New Orleans tradition as colorful as Mardi Gras, riverboats, and all that jazz!

3/4 cup chopped onion
1 clove garlic, minced
2 tablespoons butter or
  margarine
1 can (28 ounces) crushed
  tomatoes
1 can (13 3/4 ounces)
  chicken broth
1 cup water
1 teaspoon chili powder
1/2 teaspoon thyme
1/2 teaspoon salt

1/2 teaspoon sugar
1 bay leaf, crumbled
1 cup long-grain rice
1 can (12 ounces) SPAM,
  cubed
1/2 pound shrimp, cooked,
  shelled, and deveined
1 large green pepper,
  seeded and cut into
  thin rings
1/4 cup pitted black
  olives, halved

In large pot, sauté onion and garlic in butter until tender, stirring often. Add tomatoes, broth, water, chili powder, thyme, salt, sugar, and bay leaf. Bring to a boil; stir in rice and SPAM. Cover and simmer 15 minutes or until rice is tender. Add shrimp, peppers, and olives; cover and simmer 5 minutes longer. Remove bay leaf before serving.

Sunshine Ham

6 Servings

A centerpiece that glows with party excitement.

1 can (11 ounces) mandarin
  orange sections
1 package (8 ounces) cream
  cheese, softened
1/4 teaspoon grated orange
  peel

1 1/2 pound Hormel
  Canned Ham
Maraschino cherries
Thin green pepper
  strips

Drain oranges reserving 2 tablespoons syrup. Thoroughly blend together cream cheese, reserved syrup, and orange peel until well mixed. Place ham on serving plate; frost with cream cheese mixture. Arrange orange sections on frosting to make flower petals; add a cherry center. Finish with green pepper "stems." Decorate platter with remaining orange sections. Cover and refrigerate until serving time.

Pizza Olé

6 to 8 Servings

A pizza with lots of pizzazz!

1 can (15 ounces) Hormel
  Chili - No Beans
2 ready-to-bake pizza
  crusts
1 can (15 ounces) Hormel
  Tamales
Chopped green peppers

Chopped red peppers
Chopped black or
  stuffed green olives
Sliced green onions
Sliced mushrooms
Shredded Monterey
  Jack cheese

Spread chili over top of pizza crusts. Remove papers from tamales; slice tamales into bite-size pieces. Place tamales on pizzas and sprinkle with peppers, olives, onions, and mushrooms as desired. Sprinkle generously with cheese. Bake in 425°F oven about 10 minutes, or until cheese melts.

Lasagna

8 Servings

Come over for supper! No day's too busy for this easy lasagna.

1 pound lasagna noodles
8 ounces mozzarella cheese
1 can (12 ounces) SPAM,
  finely chopped
1 jar (14 ounces) marinara
  sauce, divided

1 container (15 ounces)
  ricotta cheese
1 egg, slightly beaten
2 tablespoons grated
  Parmesan cheese

Cook lasagna noodles according to package directions; drain. While lasagna is cooking, grate mozzarella cheese; reserve 1/2 cup. In mixing bowl, combine mozzarella cheese and SPAM. Reserve 1/2 cup marinara sauce. Add remaining sauce, ricotta cheese, and egg to SPAM mixture; mix well. Spread 2 tablespoons reserved sauce over bottom of 12×9×2-inch baking pan. Arrange 1/4 of the noodles over sauce; spread evenly with 1/3 of SPAM mixture. Repeat layers ending with lasagna noodles. Spread reserved sauce over top. Combine reserved mozzarella cheese with Parmesan cheese; sprinkle over top. Bake in 375°F oven 40 minutes. Let stand 10 minutes before cutting into squares.

Stuffed Flank Steak Verona   6 Servings

For a company dinner — the pleasure of rolled, stuffed steak.

1 can (7 ounces) SPAM, finely chopped
1 medium onion, finely chopped
3 cloves garlic, finely chopped
1 cup chopped parsley sprigs
3 tablespoons dry bread crumbs, finely chopped
2 tablespoons grated Parmesan cheese
1/4 teaspoon dry mustard
Pepper
1 flank steak (1 1/2 to 2 pounds), pounded to even thickness
1 tablespoon olive or cooking oil
Salt
1 can (16 ounces) Italian plum tomatoes, crushed
1/2 cup dry red wine
1/2 teaspoon basil
1/4 teaspoon oregano

Combine SPAM, onion, garlic, parsley, bread crumbs, cheese, mustard, and 1/8 teaspoon pepper. Spread mixture on flank steak; roll up jelly-roll fashion from short end. Fasten with string at 1-inch intervals; tie once or twice around lengthwise. Heat oil in large pot; brown steak well on all sides. Sprinkle with salt. Combine tomatoes with wine, basil, oregano, and pepper to taste; pour over meat. Bring to a boil; lower heat and simmer, covered, about 1 3/4 to 2 hours, or until tender. Remove from pan; let stand 15 minutes before slicing. If sauce is thin, boil gently, uncovered, to reduce to desired consistency. Serve with rigatoni or rice.

Favorite Meatloaf   8 Servings

Guests will applaud this enticing new version.

1 can (12 ounces) SPAM
1 pound ground chuck
1 medium onion, chopped
1/3 cup chopped green pepper
1/4 cup chopped parsley
1 clove garlic, minced
1/4 teaspoon salt
1/8 teaspoon pepper
2 eggs
1/3 cup dry bread crumbs

Grind SPAM or process in food processor using chopping blade. Combine with remaining ingredients; mix well. Shape into loaf. Place on rack in baking pan; bake in 375°F oven 1 hour. Let stand 5 minutes before slicing.

Double Pork Loaf

8 Servings

A moist loaf that slices beautifully and glitters with glazed pineapple.

1 medium onion, chopped
1/2 cup chopped celery
2 tablespoons butter or
   margarine
1 can (12 ounces) SPAM
1 pound ground pork
1 1/2 cups (3 slices) fresh
   bread crumbs
1/4 teaspoon salt

1/4 teaspoon poultry
   seasoning
1/8 teaspoon pepper
1 egg
1 can (8 ounces) pine-
   apple slices in syrup
2 tablespoons light
   brown sugar

In medium skillet, sauté onion and celery in butter until tender. Grind SPAM or process in food processor until finely chopped. Combine SPAM, vegetables, pork, bread crumbs, salt, poultry seasoning, pepper, and egg in bowl. Drain pineapple reserving syrup; add 1/4 cup syrup to SPAM mixture. Mix well. Pack into 9×5-inch loaf pan. Bake in 350°F oven 1 hour. Remove from oven; increase temperature to 400°F. Pour off juices; invert onto oven-proof platter. Halve pineapple slices; arrange on top of pork loaf. Combine brown sugar and 1 tablespoon pineapple syrup; brush over pineapple slices. Return to oven for 5 minutes. Spoon drippings over loaf. Let stand 5 mintues before slicing.

Nice to know: This dish can be made using two cans of SPAM instead of the ground pork.

Stuffed Italian Peppers   4 to 6 Servings

A standing invitation — fried peppers filled with saucy bravura!

1   medium onion, chopped
1   clove garlic, minced
    Cooking oil
1   can (8 ounces) tomato
    sauce
1   can (7 ounces) SPAM,
    finely chopped
1/4 cup pitted black olives,
    chopped

1   tablespoon capers,
    chopped
1/4 teaspoon basil
1   loaf (1 pound) day-old
    Italian bread
1   pound (12 to 14) small
    Italian sweet peppers

In medium saucepan, sauté onion and garlic in 1 tablespoon oil. Stir in tomato sauce, SPAM, olives, capers, and basil. Bring to a boil; lower heat and simmer, uncovered, 15 minutes to thicken slightly. Remove from heat; cool to room temperature. Halve bread lengthwise; pull out center in chunks. Add bread chunks to SPAM mixture; mix thoroughly. Wash and seed peppers; fill with SPAM-bread mixture. Using crusts of bread, cut small rounds to "cork" stuffed peppers. Heat 1/4-inch oil in large skillet; sauté peppers over medium heat until browned on all sides. Drain on paper towels. Serve hot or at room temperature.

The Quickest of the Quick

Too busy to cook? Too hot to fuss? Eager to take off for a campsite or beach? All good reasons to stock up on the convenience of Hormel food products and keep these recipes handy. In a matter of minutes, you can be savoring Beef Stew Bonanza, Turkey Romanoff, or Tamale-Chili Casserole. When the campfire's ready, you'll all be ready for Fiesta Chili, Red Flannel Hash, or Campers' Macaroni and Cheese. And at the end of a long day, nothing will taste better than fast Spanish Rice, Mexicale Hash, or creamy Chicken à la King.

Red Flannel Hash   4 Servings

An old New England mainstay in a new guise.

1 medium onion, chopped
2 tablespoons cooking oil
1 can (12 ounces) SPAM, diced
4 medium potatoes, cooked and diced

Pepper to taste
1 can (16 ounces) diced beets, drained

In large skillet, sauté onion in oil until lightly browned, stirring often. Add SPAM and potatoes; sauté 5 minutes stirring often. Sprinkle with pepper. Add beets; stir to mix. Cover and cook over low heat 10 minutes. Uncover and cook 5 minutes longer.

Microwave directions: In 10-inch square baking pan combine onion and oil. Microwave 3 minutes. Add remaining ingredients; stir to mix well. Microwave 3 minutes. Stir and microwave 3 minutes longer.

Stew Français

3 Servings

Meatballs simmered with the special ingredients of a French country stew!

1 can (24 ounces) Dinty
   Moore Meatball Stew
1 can (8 ounces) small whole
   onions, drained
1 jar (4 ounces) sliced
   mushrooms, drained

1/2 cup tomato sauce
2 tablespoons dry red
   wine
1 tablespoon Worcester-
   shire sauce

In medium saucepan, combine stew, onions, mushrooms, tomato sauce, wine and Worcestershire; heat to serving temperature. Serve with French bread or rolls, if desired.

Microwave directions: Combine all ingredients in 1 1/2-quart casserole. Cover and microwave 5 minutes.

Hungarian Stew

2 to 3 Servings

Lightly spiced stew on a bed of noodles — a mouth-watering sight!

1 can (24 ounces) Dinty
   Moore Beef Stew
1 tablespoon paprika

Poppyseed Noodles
   (below)

In medium saucepan, combine stew and paprika. Cook over medium heat, stirring constantly, until bubbly hot. Serve over poppyseed noodles.

Poppyseed Noodles: Cook egg noodles according to package directions. Toss with 1 or 2 tablespoons poppyseeds.

Meatballs 'n Dumplings

3 Servings

Meatballs and dumplings — guaranteed "appeteasers!"

1 can (24 ounces) Dinty Moore
   Meatball Stew
1 cup biscuit mix

1/3 cup milk
2 tablespoons snipped
   parsley

In medium saucepan, heat stew to bubbling. Stir biscuit mix, milk, and parsley into a soft dough; drop dough by spoonfuls onto hot stew. Cook uncovered 10 minutes; cover and cook 10 minutes more.

Baked SPAM

4 Servings

This tangy recipe has been featured on our label for years.

1 can (12 ounces) SPAM
   Whole cloves
1/3 cup firmly-packed brown
   sugar

1 teaspoon water
1 teaspoon prepared
   mustard
1/2 teaspoon vinegar.

Place SPAM on rack in shallow baking pan. Score surface; stud with cloves. Combine sugar, water, mustard, and vinegar, stirring until smooth. Brush over SPAM. Bake in 375°F oven 20 minutes basting often. Slice to serve.

Mexicale Hash

2 to 3 Servings

A winning one-pot dinner at home or on the road.

1/4 cup chopped onion
1/4 cup chopped green pepper
1 tablespoon cooking oil
1 can (15 ounces) Mary
   Kitchen Roast Beef Hash
1 can (7 ounces) whole-
   kernel corn, drained

1 cup coarsely-broken
   tortilla chips
1/2 cup shredded Monterey
   Jack cheese

In large skillet, sauté onion and green pepper in oil until tender. Add hash and corn; cook over medium heat, stirring until hot (about 5 minutes). Sprinkle with tortilla chips and cheese. Place under broiler about 2 minutes to melt cheese.

Campfire Fried Rice

4 Servings

Gather 'round for a seasoned rice surprise.

1 package (7 ounces)
   precooked rice
2 cups boiling water
1 can (7 ounces) SPAM, diced

1 envelope (1 ounce)
   fried rice seasoning
   mix

Place rice in small bowl; pour boiling water over. Cover and let stand 5 minutes. Fluff with a fork. Mix in SPAM and seasoning mix. Transfer mixture to medium skillet. Cook over medium heat 5 minutes, stirring often.

Tamale-Chili Casserole
6 Servings

Mix, bake, and serve this attractive casserole in the same dish.

1 can (15 ounces) Hormel
    Chili with Beans
1 can (15 ounces) Hormel
    Tamales

3 tablespoons chopped
    onion
1/2 cup grated Cheddar
    cheese

Spread chili in 11×7-inch baking pan. Remove paper from tamales; place tamales on chili. Sprinkle with onion and cheese. Bake in 350°F oven 30 minutes.

Microwave directions: Place chili in 1 1/2-quart casserole. Top with tamales; sprinkle with onion. Microwave 4 minutes. Sprinkle with cheese; microwave 3 minutes more. Cover and let stand 3 minutes.

Enchiladas
6 to 8 Servings

Tortillas stuffed and baked with a delicious kidney bean filling.

1 medium onion, chopped
1 clove garlic, minced
    Cooking oil
2 teaspoons chili powder
1 can (12 ounces) SPAM,
    diced
1 can (16 ounces) kidney
    beans, drained

12 tortillas, canned,
    frozen, or refrigerated
1 can (10 ounces)
    enchilada sauce
1 cup shredded Monterey
    Jack cheese

In medium saucepan, sauté onion and garlic in 1 tablespoon oil until tender. Stir in chili powder; cook and stir 1 minute longer. Mix in SPAM and kidney beans; reserve. To assemble enchiladas, sauté tortillas in oil for 1 minute on each side; drain on paper toweling. Put about 1/4 cup SPAM filling on each tortilla; roll up. Place in lightly-greased 12×9-inch baking pan, seam side down. Pour enchilada sauce over filled tortillas; sprinkle with cheese. Bake in 350°F oven 30 minutes.

Sauerkraut Stew

2 or 3 Servings

All the gusto of beef and sauerkraut.

1 can (24 ounces) Dinty
   Moore Beef Stew

1 can (8 ounces)
   sauerkraut, drained

In medium saucepan, combine stew and sauerkraut. Cook over medium heat, stirring constantly, until bubbly hot.

Turkey Romanoff

3 Servings

Easy preparation in a fancy disguise.

1 package (5 1/2 ounces)
   noodles and Romanoff
   sauce mix
1/2 teaspoon salt
1 can (6 3/4 ounces) Hormel
   Chunk Turkey

2 tablespoons instant
   nonfat dry milk
2 tablespoons butter
   or margarine
1 can (4 ounces) sliced
   mushrooms, drained

Remove sauce mix from package; set aside. Cook noodles with salt in 6 cups boiling water 7 minutes; drain. Drain turkey, reserving broth. Add water to broth to make 1/3 cup; stir in milk. In same saucepan, combine butter, milk mixture, mushrooms, noodles, and sauce mix. Break up turkey with a fork; add to saucepan. Cook and stir until hot.

Beef Stew Bonanza

10 servings

When you're hungry for a potful of big, big flavor.

1 can (40 ounces) Dinty
   Moore Beef Stew

3 cans (15 ounces each)
   Hormel Chili with
   Beans

Combine stew and chili in large pot. Heat over medium heat, stirring occasionally, until just boiling. Serve with hot garlic bread, if desired.

Chicken à la King

4 servings

Convenient enough for a camping meal, or a busy-day break at home.

1 can (6 3/4 ounces) Hormel
   Chunk Chicken
1 envelope à la king sauce
   mix

1 can (8 ounces) green
   beans, drained

Drain chicken reserving juices. Add water to juices to make 1 cup. In small saucepan, combine sauce mix and juice mixture. Heat and stir over medium heat until sauce boils and thickens. Break up chicken with a fork; add to sauce with green beans. Cook and stir until hot. Serve over hot rice.

Deep Dish Beef Pie

5 to 6 Servings

Savory stew sealed in a biscuit crust.

1 can (40 ounces) Dinty
   Moore Beef Stew
1 cup biscuit mix

1 teaspoon celery seed
1/4 cup water

Pour stew into ungreased 2-quart casserole. Mix biscuit mix, celery seed, and water to make a soft dough. Roll out on lightly-floured surface and shape to fit top of casserole. Place dough on stew; cut a few slits in top. Bake in 425°F oven 20 to 25 minutes, or until lightly browned.

Yam-Pineapple Casserole   4 Servings

Equally fine for a Saturday-night supper or a Sunday-dinner side dish.

1 can (20 ounces) crushed
   pineapple in syrup
1 can (12 ounces) SPAM
1 can (17 ounces) yams,
   drained

2 tablespoons pancake
   syrup
1 tablespoon butter or
   margarine
2 cloves

Drain pineapple, reserving 1/3 cup syrup. Spread pineapple over bottom of lightly-greased, 1-quart baking dish. Cut SPAM into 4 slices; overlap slices on top of pineapple. Place yams around SPAM. In small saucepan, heat reserved pineapple syrup, pancake syrup, butter, and cloves until butter is melted. Spoon 1/3 sauce over casserole. Bake in 375°F oven 30 minutes, basting with remaining sauce after 10 and 20 minutes.

Microwave directions: In 2-cup measure combine 1/3 cup pineapple syrup, pancake syrup, butter, and cloves; microwave 2 minutes. Reserve. Assemble casserole in 1 1/2-quart baking dish; pour 1/2 sauce mixture over top. Microwave 4 minutes. Pour remaining sauce over top; microwave 3 minutes more.

Speedy Chinese Stir-fry   2 Servings

You'll fool everyone with the authentic taste of this easy Oriental medley.

1 package (10 ounces) frozen
   Chinese-style stir-
   fry vegetables
1 cup shredded cabbage
2 tablespoons chopped green
   onions

2 tablespoons cooking oil
1 can (7 ounces) SPAM,
   diced
1/4 cup water

Heat 10- or 11-inch skillet until very hot. Remove seasoning packet from vegetables. Spread vegetables, cabbage, and onions over bottom of skillet. Pour oil evenly over vegetables; stir to coat pieces. Cover and cook 2 minutes, stirring once. Add SPAM; sprinkle seasonings over mixture and add water. Cook and stir about 2 minutes until serving temperature.

Stew 'n Biscuit Bake

2 to 3 Servings

Two great shortcuts — sour cream savor and baked-in-the pot biscuits.

1 can (24 ounces) Dinty Moore Beef Stew	1 cup biscuit mix
1/4 cup dairy sour cream	1/4 cup water

In 1 1/2-quart casserole, combine stew and sour cream. Bake in 425°F oven. Meanwhile, in small bowl, stir biscuit mix and water to make a soft dough. Drop by spoonfuls into hot stew. Bake about 20 minutes until biscuits are lightly browned.

Oriental Meatball Stew

3 Servings

Chinese food you can fix any night.

1 can (24 ounces) Dinty Moore Meatball Stew	3 tablespoons soy sauce
1 can (8 ounces) sliced water chestnuts, drained	Hot cooked rice
	Chow mein noodles

In medium saucepan, combine stew, water chestnuts, and soy sauce; heat over medium heat, stirring occasionally. Serve over hot rice and garnish with chow mein noodles.

Stew 'n Dumplings

6 Servings

Vegetable variations and fluffy dumplings add up to quick satisfaction.

1 can (40 ounces) Dinty Moore Beef Stew	2/3 cup milk
2 cups biscuit mix	2 tablespoons finely-chopped parsley

In large skillet or pot, heat stew to bubbling. In bowl, stir biscuit mix, milk, and parsley to make a soft dough. Drop dough by spoonfuls onto hot stew. Cook, uncovered, over low heat 10 minutes. Cover and cook 10 minutes more.

Variations:

Add 1 can (16 ounces) mixed vegetables, drained
Add 1 can (4 1/2 ounces) mushroom slices, drained
Add 1 can (8 ounces) tomato sauce

South of the Border Stew   6 Servings

Corn, red peppers, and seasoning add a lively Mexican touch.

1 can (40 ounces) Dinty Moore
   Beef Stew
1 can (12 ounces) whole-
   kernel corn with red
   peppers, drained

1 teaspoon taco sauce
   Corn chips

In medium saucepan, combine stew, corn, and taco sauce; heat to serving temperature. Sprinkle with corn chips and serve.

Note: You may want to substitute 1 tablespoon chili powder for taco sauce.

Change-of-Pace Beans   2 Servings

Simple addition multiplies goodness.

1 can (7 1/2 ounces) Hormel
   Beans 'n Wieners

1 can (7 1/2 ounces)
   Hormel Beans 'n Bacon

In small saucepan, combine Beans 'n Wieners with Beans 'n Bacon. Cook and stir until mixture comes to a boil.

Caliente Chili Bake

6 Servings

Hot stuff! Tamales baked with chili and topped with corn chips.

- 1 can (15 ounces) Hormel Chili with Beans
- 1 can (10 3/4 ounces) condensed cream of chicken soup
- 1 can (12 ounces) whole-kernel corn, drained
- 1 can (15 ounces) Hormel Tamales
- 1/2 cup shredded Cheddar cheese
- Corn chips

Combine chili, soup, and corn in 11×7-inch baking dish. Remove papers from tamales and place on top of chili mixture. Sprinkle cheese over center of tamales. Bake in 350°F oven 20 minutes. Sprinkle with corn chips and bake 5 to 10 minutes more.

Microwave directions: Combine chili, soup, and corn in baking dish; top with tamales as above. Microwave 6 minutes. Sprinkle with cheese; top with corn chips. Microwave 5 minutes. Cover and let stand 3 minutes.

Fancy Stew

4 Servings

Beef stew with a gourmet French accent.

- 1 can (40 ounces) Dinty Moore Beef Stew
- 1 cup drained canned whole onions
- 1/4 cup dry red wine

Combine all ingredients in medium saucepan; bring to a boil. Lower heat and simmer, covered 5 minutes to blend flavors. Serve with buttered noodles and rye bread, if desired.

Note: Toss poppyseeds with noodles for extra flavor and variety.

Corned Beef 'n Cabbage Hash

2 Servings

A classic flavor combo prepared in just 10 minutes.

2 cups chopped cabbage
1 teaspoon prepared mustard
1/2 teaspoon caraway seeds
2 tablespoons butter or
  margarine

1 can (15 ounces) Mary
  Kitchen Corned Beef
  Hash
Pepper to taste

In large skillet, sauté cabbage, mustard, and caraway in butter 3 minutes, stirring often. Break up hash and add to skillet. Cook and stir about 5 minutes until hot and slightly browned. Season with pepper to taste.

Fiesta Chili

4 to 6 Servings

Chili, tamales, and tomatoes team up in a great-tasting main course.

1 can (15 ounces) Hormel
  Chili with Beans
1 can (16 ounces) tomatoes,
  cut up

1 can (15 ounces)
  Hormel Tamales
Cheddar cheese,
  shredded

Combine chili and tomatoes in medium saucepan. Remove papers from tamales; slice into bite-size pieces; gently stir into chili. Heat over low heat until hot, stirring occasionally. Serve with a garnish of cheese.

Mexican Supper

4 Servings

Unbelievably good any time, from brunch to midnight snacks.

1 can (15 ounces) Hormel
  Tamales

1 can (15 ounces)
  Hormel Chili-
  No Beans

Remove papers from tamales. Heat tamales gently in small saucepan. Place on warm serving platter or on 4 warm plates. Heat chili in same saucepan; pour over tamales.

Campers' Macaroni and Cheese

4 Servings

A favorite blend enriched with whole-meal nourishment.

1 package (7 1/4 ounces)
    macaroni and cheese mix
1/2 teaspoon salt
6 cups boiling water
1/4 cup butter or margarine
1/4 cup water

2 tablespoons instant
    nonfat dry milk
1 can (5 ounces) Hormel
    Vienna Sausages,
    cut up
1 can (8 ounces) carrots
    and peas, drained

Remove cheese sauce mix from package; set aside. Cook macaroni with salt in boiling water about 7 minutes or until tender; drain. Return macaroni to pot. Add butter, water, milk, and cheese sauce mix; stir until smooth. Mix in Vienna Sausages and vegetables; cook, to serving temperature, stirring constantly.

Spanish Rice

6 Servings

Kids love this easy skillet casserole.

1 package (7 1/2 ounces)
    Spanish rice mix
2 tablespoons butter or
    margarine

2 cups boiling water
1 can (16 ounces)
    tomatoes, broken up
1 can (12 ounces) SPAM

Remove seasoning envelope from rice package; set aside. In large skillet, sauté rice in butter until lightly browned, stirring often. Pour in water; stir in seasoning mixture. Add tomatoes; bring to a boil. Cut SPAM into 6 slices; overlap atop rice mixture. Cover and simmer about 15 minutes, until rice is tender and liquid absorbed.

Index

Find Your Favorite Hormel Product